The 2x2 Manager

John Dembitz

Thorogood Publishing Ltd
10-12 Rivington Street
London EC2A 3DU
Telephone: 020 7749 4748

Email: info@thorogoodpublishing.co.uk
Web: www.thorogoodpublishing.co.uk

A CIP catalogue record for this book is available
from the British Library.

Paperback ISBN: (10) 1854188364
(13) 9781854188366

Ebook ISBN: (10) 1854188372 (13) 9781854188373

Printed and bound in Great Britain by
Marston Book Services Limited, Oxfordshire

Critical acclaim for *The 2x2 Manager* and John Dembitz:

"John Dembitz's perceptive book is a practical how-to manual for the thoughtful manager. He shows how the systematic application of 2x2 thinking clarifies choices and helps balance competing (and sometimes conflicting) objectives. His advice on how to manage employee relationships, product-market evaluation methods, and traditional SWOT analysis all provide a vital primer for the experienced – and not so experienced – business director. The 2x2 Manager will help business leaders at any of the growth stages it identifies: and hopefully enable them to avoid the pitfalls Dembitz cites.

The 2x2 Manager draws on established management concepts – the Prisoner's Dilemma, Boston Consulting Group's Growth-Share analysis, the Johari window – with a host of fresh and contemporary anecdotal case studies. The book is an easy and rewarding read."

Simon Walker, Director General, Institute of Directors

"We have used 2x2 matrices with John to enormous advantage and in a number of situations and groups in our professional property service business – like Ronseal 'The 2x2 Manager' does what it says on the tin – simple and very effective!"

Carl Whayman, Group CEO, Lee Baron Group Ltd

"If you can find a book that will provide you one idea that you can use once, you've done well. 'The 2x2 Manager' provides a great idea that you can use forever."

John Neill, Chairman and CEO, Unipart Group of Companies

"John Dembitz has put together a highly valuable and easy-to-understand explanation of 2x2 matrices and their powerful applications. This is an analytical tool that should be utilized much more frequently in the business world; drawing on his own experience and other real-life examples, Dembitz's book gives managers a clear 'when, how and why' to create one and use it to the best effect."

Nick Shreiber, Chairman, Nick Shreiber & Associates, LLC

"This book should win the KISS award: Keep It Simple, Stupid. A valuable handbook for the business person who is thinking about business strategy and so much more. It will help focus your analytical thinking and allow you to make decisions with more confidence."

David Tyler, Chairman of J. Sainsbury plc, Chairman of Hammerson plc and a Non-Executive Director of Burberry Group plc

Table of Contents

2X2 MANAGER

To my wife Alexandra, children Robert and Sarah, and daughter-in-law Heather... for your inspiration and support!

2X2 MANAGER

Introduction

Over the past 16 years as non-executive chairman of a wide range of entrepreneurial businesses, largely described as small to medium sized enterprises (SMEs), I have had the pleasure of interacting with a diverse group of successful entrepreneurs and business leaders, and their executive teams.

Usually within the first three months of being appointed as non-executive chairman I request (and, if appropriate, require) that the senior executive team (usually board members) go off-site for a strategic review. This strategic review is typically 'facilitated' by me, given that I have the training and experience to do so. Apart from the strategic insights that such a session can deliver, from a purely personal perspective, I find them of immense value as they provide an extraordinary opportunity to gain a highly accelerated insight into the company, and the executives - both as individuals and as a team. And, to be fair, they also provide a fairly rapid exposure of me to the executive team. All in all such an event helps to bond the senior team together, and create significant insights and understanding about the business, where it is and where it's going, including the all important question of 'how are we going to get there?' Or, to put it another way, to determine the 'To be'; the 'As is' and then the steps and actions that need to be taken to get from one to the other.

Looking back over the past 16 years I cannot think of a single time when at some stage during the strategy away-day I did not draw a 2x2 matrix to explain/illustrate/ demonstrate how best to think through an issue. Irrespective of whether it was with a company turning over £3m or £300m; irrespective of whether it was a small cap quoted or private company; irrespective of whether it was a professional management team put together by a private equity backer or the original entrepreneur, the reaction was the same: 'WOW!... that's so terrific, so simple, how come no one has shown stuff like this to us before?!'

But then this reaction is not that surprising. SMEs tend to be entrepreneurial businesses. Many with the original founder still very much in control. Many with substantially the core team still in place, and expanded over time. These are not businesses that typically engage consulting firms or hire business school graduates. They are therefore not exposed to some of these techniques, despite many of them having been around for decades.

Most recently I was advising a relatively small wholly owned subsidiary of a very substantial, multi-billion dollar, quoted, global corporation. And to my surprise they had not come across any of the 2x2s contained in this book, with the exception of SWOT.

Larger companies have management consultants crawling all over them from time to time; mid to larger cap companies frequently hire business school graduates; both management consultants and business school graduates would have come across 2x2 matrices and their applications and would be inclined to pass on their knowledge to their clients/employers.

I experienced this 'WOW' reaction so many times to a number of different 2x2s from diverse groups of owner/managers that I decided to do something about it.

This little book, 'The 2x2 Manager', is the result!

Having explored the internet to see the existing material that's available on this topic I was further motivated to write this book. Of course, when inputting '2x2 matrices' into Google thousands of pages are immediately made available but in my opinion the topic is over theorised and over complicated. What I wanted to do, as I have done many times on various away days, is to introduce the concept of 2x2s, their diversity, their simplicity and their terrific power to simplify the complex. I have therefore no intention of over complicating in the pages that follow.

I absolutely have no desire to suggest that the few ideas contained within this book are either original or the equivalent of management elixir. They are exactly what they are: complex ideas made simple; constructed to facilitate the analysis of complex issues in an easily digestible manner.

I have used every effort to trace and provide acknowledgement to the creators of each of the matrices contained in the following pages. This, however, has not been possible for all of them. Despite extensive research the creator has not been identified on all occasions and for that omission I take full responsibility. If further information should be made available then attribution will be given in any subsequent editions.

If I have oversimplified that is good. The power is in usage.

The only criteria of success of this book is whether you, the reader, will now go forth and use any of the five 2x2 matrices detailed in the pages to come or, better still, create your own.

2X2 MANAGER

Chapter 1
What is a 2x2 Matrix?

The application of 2x2 matrices is a simple process to facilitate thinking and decision-making. A 2x2 helps in organising events, decisions, facts, data, values, tangibles and intangibles in such a way that clarifies, segments, simplifies and helps to make sense. They help to create order out of chaos; to differentiate the possible from the impossible; to highlight ranges of related risk to various options.

If you know what a 2x2 matrix is and how it works, then skip to the beginning of the next chapter.

Imagine four boxes lying on the floor arranged as two and then two again.

We have just constructed a 2x2. Now imagine rather than boxes they were just simple squares linked together.

If we were to apply vertical and horizontal axes, we can start to provide some framework to our boxes/squares as per below:

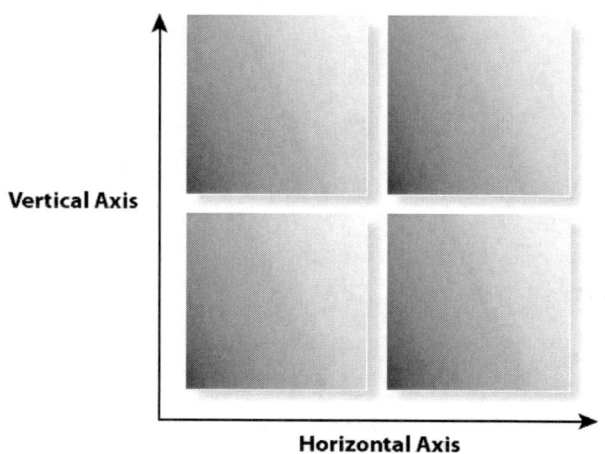

Vertical Axis

Horizontal Axis

We can now start to consider what we have constructed by applying labels. For instance we could label the vertical axis as PEOPLE, and the horizontal axis as TEMPERAMENT. We can go one step further and sub-divide PEOPLE into MALE and FEMALE; and TEMPERAMENT into HAPPY and SAD, thereby creating the following matrix:

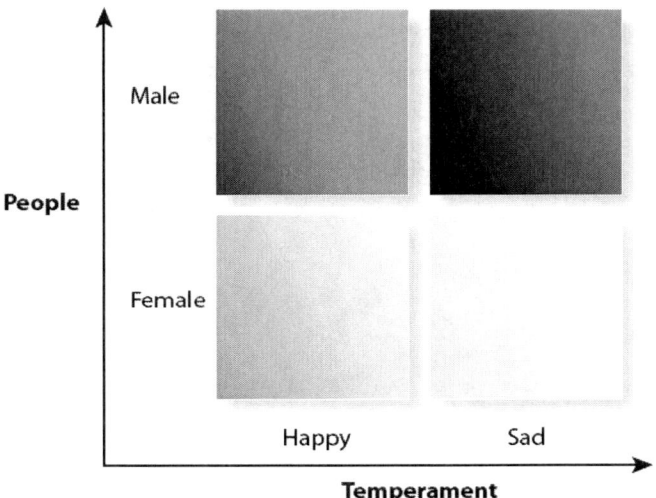

We have created a 2x2. We can now identify the top left square as representing happy males; the bottom left square as representing happy females; the top right square for sad males; and the bottom right square for sad females.

We can vary the axis by applying a scale from Low to High; for example we could label the vertical CONTENTMENT, with Low at the bottom and High at the top, and the horizontal WEALTH, with Small to Large being the scales left to right. Hence we have:

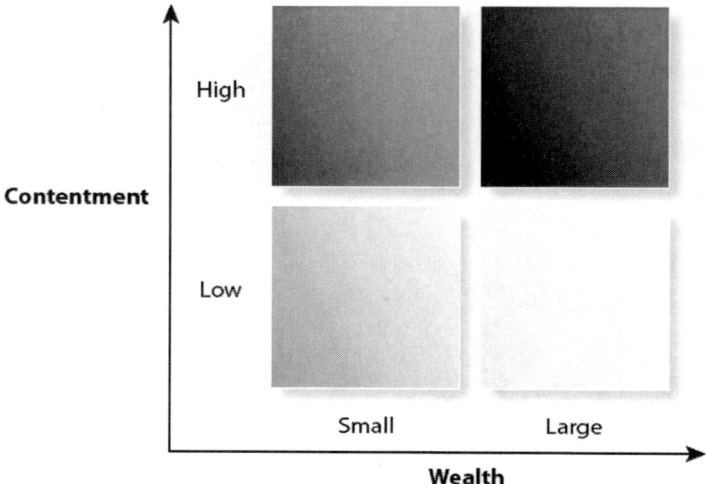

We can thereby segment groups into those with small wealth and low contentment (bottom left), large wealth and high contentment (top right), small wealth and high contentment (top left) and low contentment but large wealth (bottom right).

In itself this is of little value but applied to certain situations being able to segment in such an easy manner can be of immense help to get to a solution.

The axes can of course be labelled in an unlimited number of ways and so can the sub-segments as per the vertical and horizontal squares, subject to there being independent variables. This provides us with a vast number of different uses, which we shall explore in the coming chapters.

It is the very simplicity of 2x2s that make them so valuable and user friendly but before progressing to the next chapter why don't you try to construct your own 2x2 for whatever may be relevant to you? Think about the dimension (the vertical and horizontal axes), think about the sub-segments/units, and proceed to create your own. There really are unlimited options:

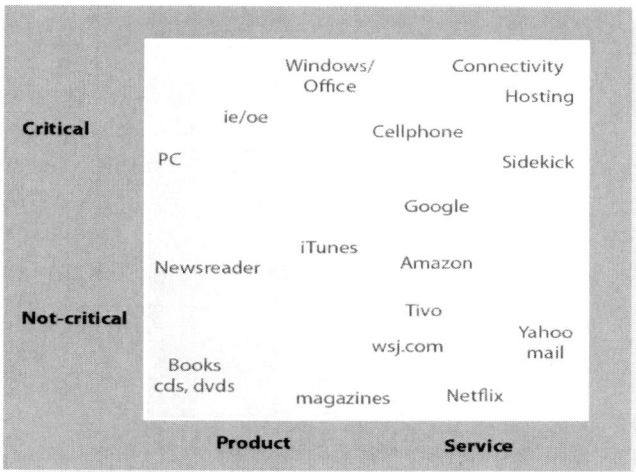

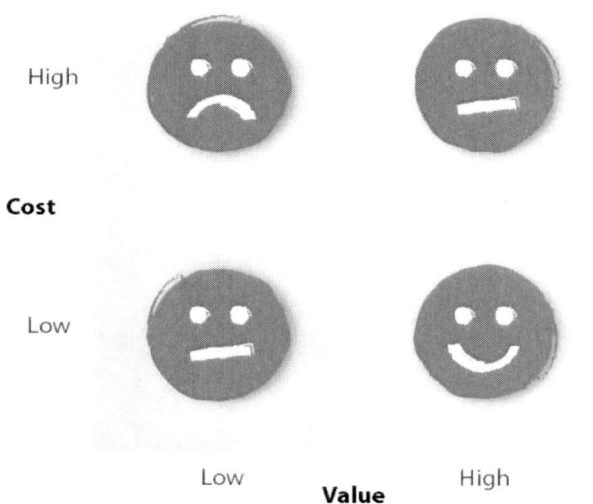

I suggest you take a look at the following link on Google just to get a sense of the vast array of possibilities:

https://www.google.co.uk/search?q=2x2+matrix

The application of 2x2s is only limited by your imagination.

In reality 2x2s have become recognised for their power and ability to move management thinking and action. Perhaps the most notable recognition of the power and influence of 2x2s is the re-branding of a well-known corporation, EMAP plc, to the 'Top Right Group Limited'. This was not undertaken by some starry-eyed designer for the sake of 'change' but by hard-nosed private equity owners who understood the power of gaining alignment to being seen as a growth business. The top-right hand square being where most high performing, high growth businesses aspire to be in the classic portfolio analysis matrix. (See chapter 6: Boston Consulting Group's Growth-Share Matrix.)

Chapter 2
How Can 2x2s Be Used?

2x2 matrices are applicable in a number of different ways, the four most frequently used are:

1. **Progression**, in which one of my favourite applications called Johari's Window, sits. (See chapter 3.) It is an application that is relevant to organisations and individuals alike.

2. **Situation Analysis,** which has one of the best-known and most frequently used applications, the classic SWOT (Strength, Weakness, Opportunities and Threats) analysis (see chapter 5). Situation analysis is also appropriate for undertaking product/market analyses to determine product/market and market entry strategies.

3. **Decision Support**, as for example the well-known Boston Consulting Group's Growth-Share Matrix (see chapter 6). This aims to show the relationship between market growth and market share, as it relates to the various units within an organisation, or within a portfolio of investments.

4. **Classification**, by which a vast number of diverse facts can be collated and classified into simple 'containers'. For example, in performance assessment the entire employee pool can be classified into defined segments - for example secure/high-performer; secure/low-performer; insecure/high-performer; insecure/low-performer. Once segmented, actions can be developed as appropriate.

We will now look at a few of these in greater detail to illustrate the ease of application and to demonstrate the immense value that can be derived from this simple methodology. Once understood, 2x2s can facilitate analytical thinking, can speed up decision-making and generally help to simplify what often appear to be complex situations.

To me, a basic understanding of some of the more important and frequently used 2x2 matrices is all that is required for most people to get to grips with the power of the format. Once understood, the application of 2x2 matrices is limited only by the imagination of the individual and no structured textbook is either necessary or particularly helpful. (If you would like to explore further I would recommend the definitive book on 2x2s written by Alex Lowy and Phil Hood, 'The Power of the 2x2 Matrix: Using 2x2 Thinking to Solve Business Problems and Make Better Decisions', Jossey Bass Business and Management Series.)

As I have already mentioned, the application is appropriate both in a professional and a personal capacity. 2x2 matrices can help understand and resolve business and personal issues. This is exactly why I shall take a much closer look at Johari's Window in the next chapter, a 2x2 that spans all the categories.

Why should a small business book like this make any reference to non-business applications? For one reason I believe it is impossible to draw a line that separates 100% one's business and personal life; secondly, business is essentially all about people and getting better interaction and collaboration is about having greater openness; and thirdly we are all human beings, irrespective of race, colour, creed, religion - hence anything that helps to better understand each other has got to be good.

As an aside, I have been using 2x2s for the best part of the past 40 years to help communicate certain messages, to help assess certain situations and to help evaluate, problem solve and understand complexity in an easy way. All of this I have used not only in the office, but also in the home with my family and friends.

In my previous book, '*It's the People! What really drives great management and leadership*' (LID Publishing, November 2011) I placed huge importance on communication. My love of Johari's Window is based on its massive power to enhance communication, hence in the next chapter I shall go into it in some detail. To give you just one example, I recently had lunch with someone who had been an executive director of one of the companies I chaired. He had consequently been exposed to one of my away days. He told me how applying Johari's Window had helped him to unravel a sensitive communication issue between directors that had been festering for years. That's gratifying success!

Chapter 3
Johari's Window

As already mentioned, one of my favourite forms of a 2x2 is called 'Johari's Window', named after the first names of its inventors, Joseph Luft and Harry Ingham. To me it is one of the most useful models describing the process of human interaction. Its very simplicity belies its overwhelming power.

A four panel 'window', or 2x2 matrix, as illustrated below, divides personal awareness into four different types, as represented by its four quadrants: open, hidden, blind and unknown. The lines dividing the four panels are like window shades, which can move as interaction progresses.

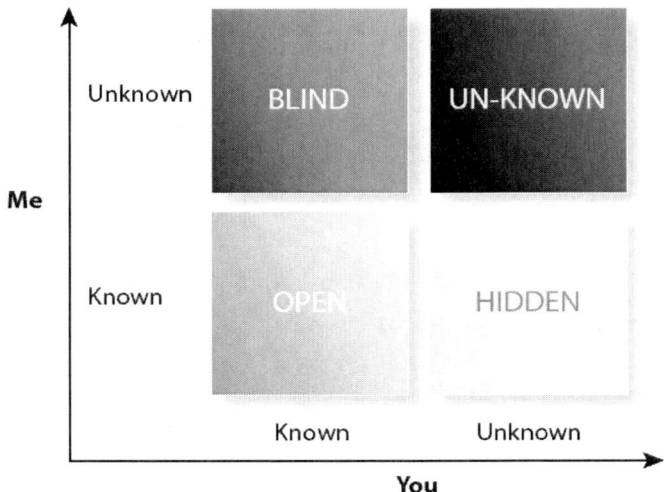

This is one of the most powerful ways to illustrate the importance of communication; real communication where there is genuine one to one discussion, eye to eye and between two people. No amount of e-mails, blogs and tweets can impact on the power of two people communicating in the same room with each other.

In any form of business environment, creating an understanding of the substance of Johari's Window can help to improve collaboration, collegiality, mutual trust and understanding and hence almost certainly productivity and profitability. There is not a shadow of doubt in my mind that many, if not most, issues in business could be effectively resolved if people were able to communicate with each other, if people were prepared to engage with each other fully rather than hiding behind impenetrable barriers, behind misapprehensions and an opaque understanding of reality, behind half truths and half articulated thoughts. So what's it all about?

As the matrix above shows there are two axes, the vertical labelled 'ME', segmented into known and unknown; and the horizontal axis labelled 'YOU', equally segmented into known and unknown.

There are, as a consequence, four squares/windows:

- The **OPEN** window can be described as a window in which both you and I share known facts. Assuming we were together in the same place, if I were wearing a blue button-down shirt without a tie both of us would KNOW that I was wearing a blue button-down shirt without a tie. Similarly if you were wearing glasses and had a moustache, I would know that too just by being in the same place as you. There are numerous facts about each other that we both know, by sight, smell, hearing and touch, and by information we may have accumulated from past meetings or briefings, reading, surfing the internet etc. It is information either essentially in the public domain or that we have been informed about. In the past decade there has been an explosion of what is available in the public domain just by 'getting on-line'. Never in the past has it been possible to unlock so much professional, business and personal information whether just by Googling a name or via the multitude of social networks, the biggest and most important being Facebook and, specifically, in the business domain, LinkedIn.

This open window is where we all are to begin with. It is the area of shared/common information and knowledge. At times it will also include assumptions that we may have made based on what may have appeared as 'shared' information, even though it may be wrong. It is usually the basis upon which communication can commence. It is where our basic understanding of each other can grow from.

• The **HIDDEN** window is one step away from shared knowledge. In this space there are things KNOWN to me, but UNKNOWN to you, or hidden from you. For example, I know that last night I had a really late closure meeting that was then celebrated by numerous glasses of champagne and as a consequence I am feeling really tired and have a slight headache. You have absolutely no idea about any of this unless we happened to have been at the closure meeting together, in which case it would be in the open square as shared knowledge. In fact, the majority of information about me is unknown to you. My feelings, my priorities, my interpretation of events, my likes and dislikes, my emotions are all unknown to you. You may make certain assumptions about them and they may be right or totally wrong. Today real care needs to be taken in respect of the information available on the various social networking websites. Not everything is either correct or true. Whilst the explosion of information that can be accessed has been astronomical, it has created great need for vigilance and care in the use of such information.

In this window there is a degree of comfort that can be had from the knowledge that there are a vast number of things that remain hidden from others until you are prepared to release specific elements. There is comfort in the knowledge that you are in control.

Let's take another situation: interviewing. The whole purpose of interviewing is to verify facts, data and information about you; to be able to gain extra insights into you through dialogue and question and answer sessions; to be able to get a better 'feel' for the type of person you are and how you react in certain situations. In other words the process of interviewing is to a certain extent getting you to reveal bits that may have been hidden or substantiating information to ensure that it is correct, appropriate and relevant to you.

Consider the world's reaction to two now notorious individuals: Julian Assange and Edward Snowden, both of whom made public vast amounts of information considered secret by the authorities and by doing so allegedly put nations at risk - they were essentially placing in the shared public domain information that was previously hidden.

– **Julian Paul Assange:** an Australian editor, activist, publisher and journalist. He is known as the editor-in-chief and founder of WikiLeaks, which publishes submissions of secret information, news leaks and classified media from anonymous news sources and whistle-blowers.

- **Edward Joseph Snowden:** an American computer specialist, a former Central Intelligence Agency (CIA) employee, and former National Security Agency (NSA) contractor who disclosed up to 1.7 million classified NSA documents to several media outlets, initiating the NSA leaks. The leaks revealed operational details of a global surveillance apparatus operated by the United States working with its Five Eyes partners, the United Kingdom, Canada, Australia and New Zealand, and intimately connected with most Western countries' security agencies.

The above can easily be plotted on our matrix showing movement from the bottom right window to the bottom left window - with all the related ramifications.

- The **BLIND** window is also one step away from shared knowledge but this time involving you. In other words there are things KNOWN to you, but UNKNOWN to me, things that I am totally blind to. You KNOW that you have a strong dislike for people wearing blue button-down shirts without a tie as it shows too high a degree of informality. You KNOW that you arrived at the meeting with a strong belief that things are going to be difficult, due to advice you had been given by others and some of the reading you had done in preparation. None of these 'facts' are KNOWN to me. I haven't got a clue about your pre-conceived ideas, and what's worse is that both of our pre-conceived ideas may all be in total conflict with each other, even though they may be totally wrong. This can add fuel to distrust and disagreement even before a single word may have been uttered.

As with the previous 'hidden window', in this 'blind window' there is a degree of comfort that can be gained from the knowledge that there are a vast number of things that remain hidden from others until you are prepared to release specific elements. There is comfort in the knowledge that you are in control.

But this may create a situation of great risk too. Consider the way that China in 2013 began to flex its muscle over the islands that Japan believes are theirs - the island cluster in the East China Sea, known as Senkaku in Japan and Diaoyu in China. What has further increased tension is that the USA has a defence treaty with Japan and they have stated clearly that (a) they believe the islands to belong to Japan and (b) that they will be prepared to support Japan if necessary. In retaliation China declared a no-fly zone over the islands, which the USA immediately ignored and sent its aircraft in defiance of the Chinese. The prevailing situation is poten-tially explosive as neither side is ready to open any of their 'windows'; they are operating on core assumptions about respective reactions which may be totally inaccurate; no normal terms of engagement seem to be in place. In other words they are operating in a blind situation with huge global risks!

• The **UNKNOWN** window is an area far away from us both. In this space we are both literally in the dark, both of us have no knowledge! This is the space which contains factors UNKNOWN by me and UNKNOWN by you. Sudden reac-tions may be stimulated by impulses from the unconscious, but this is not an area I focus on. To penetrate this space needs the specialist skills of the psychoanalyst, hence this is an area that I leave unexplored. Frankly, for most of the usual day-to-day interaction between people, colleagues or friends this is unnecessary terrain and can remain unex-plored.

That said, Donald Rumsfeld, the US defence secretary in President George W. Bush's administration, made famous the area of unknown-unknowns:

"Reports that say that something hasn't happened are always interesting to me because, as we know, there are known knowns; there are things we know we know. We also know there are known unknowns; that is to say we know there are some things we do not know. **But there are also unknown unknowns - the ones we don't know we don't know."**

So I have broadly defined each of the four possible windows. What of their importance?

Essentially, as I have stressed earlier, what Johari's Window is about is communication.

In the open window there is open communication about the shared aspects of people - all being relatively easy. This is often referred to as the water fountain chat, or the coffee machine meeting. People are happy to chat about their activities from the past weekend, their favourite football team, what they thought of the latest contestants in Strictly Come Dancing or the X Factor, and certainly during the course of the summer of 2012 how team GB performed in the Olympics, or in the winter of 2013 how Britain's cricket team managed to be totally obliterated by their Australian hosts in the Ashes, losing 5-0! They may also be happy to chat about politics in a fairly neutral manner, frustration about politician's expenses, the inability of the world's politicians to tackle climate change, or politics with a smaller 'p' related to their business and often about the boss' lack of understanding, and nearly always about the lack of communication that takes place within the business! Within this space people generally feel unthreatened and engage in dialogue in a relatively natural way like they did in the school playground, except in a more adult manner.

The nature of what is acceptable changes with time, and with society. For example, a group of close friends will openly discuss issues and aspects of their lives that acquaintances or work colleagues would not. In the Noughties, the hugely popular and successful television series 'Sex and the City', depicting the relationship between four single women in New York, illustrated this perfectly as did another American TV series, 'Friends', which depicted the relationship between three single men and three single women. The closeness of their relationship enabled a level of intimacy in their dialogue in what they were prepared to communicate with each other. In fact TV is an excellent mirror of what society was like in different ages, and what people were happy to discuss in an open forum. This is constantly evolving and changing. Equally, what people are prepared to discuss at work, or in the 'playground', evolves and changes over time. Again a good example being the hugely successful series 'Mad Men', based around an American advertising agency in the late '50s.

The nature of what is brought into this open forum changes depending on the people involved, their established relationships and prevailing morays of society. Again a phenomena that occurred in the summer of 2012 was the trilogy 'Fifty Shades of Grey' by E.L. James. These books took the UK and many other countries by storm, often described as 'mummy porn', becoming all time best sellers. They, in turn, set new standards in what (in particular) women were prepared to discuss amongst each other, specifically in terms of their own sexuality.

In the evolving world of the 21st century, there are driving forces at play that are pulling more and more 'matter' into what could be referred to as open forums. The phenomenal growth of social networks - be they primarily personal, as per Facebook, or primarily professional, as per LinkedIn - have already had an impact on society. Twitter is also having an impact, with short messages flying in all directions - "went yesterday to a restaurant, saw celebrity eating there"! Not yet really sure what segment of communication to place this in? Yes, more information is flying around cyber space; yes, people's resumes and CVs are readily available on-line and can often be accessed openly by all comers; yes, increasing volumes of information are available on everyone just by plugging into Google. And yet people are actually finding it harder and harder to communicate on a one-to-one basis. Is the skill of interpersonal relations under threat from hiding behind the screen and potential anonymity?

When I make presentations about communications I stress that e-mail is not communication. E-mail is about the transfer of information and data. Sending messages via Facebook /LinkedIn/Twitter and the thousands of other social media sites is not about communication. These exchanges share information and may be a part of the complex web that together creates effective communication but on their own they are inadequate at best, and simply dangerous at worst.

Johari's Window is all about recognising the limitations and facilitating the removal of barriers.

The hidden and blind windows contain data and information that is hidden between people - they are the spaces that contain things we know about ourselves, information that we assume about others and our non-communicated judgements, emotions, senses, situation analyses, prejudices, needs and wants. They are the 'un-saids'.

The only way any of the stuff contained in either of these spaces can be opened up is by a willingness to share the information with others. In other words to open the windows! To turn the 'un-saids' into 'saids' by enlarging the amount of shared knowledge, by enlarging the open window, by enlarging the known-known space. The only way that can be done is by converting what may be 'unknown' into 'known' by sharing information with the other person by communicating, by looking the other person in the eye and talking with them on a one-to-one basis.

I have frequently demonstrated this as follows:

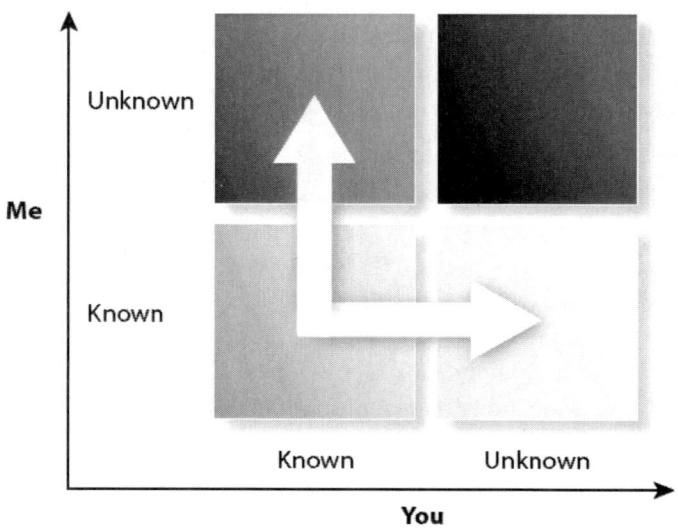

By engaging in open communication, by sharing real information with others, it is possible to significantly enlarge the shared/open space and reduce the amount of information that is kept hidden. Pushing the two axes further apart, as indicated by the arrows above, enlarges the space for shared knowledge and understanding. At the same time the amount of information left hidden/blind is reduced. The size of the window that is UNKNOWN to both you and me is also potentially reduced, subconsciously (although this is just my hypothesis, without any factual substantiation!).

As I have already mentioned, this fourth window, the top right box, is not possible to penetrate without specialist skills of psychoanalysis (or related expertise). As such I simply recognise its existence.

As depicted below, given that the total area represented by the four windows remains the same, opening the windows and exchanging information openly that previously may have been hidden or blind, in turn reduces these areas with the shared window now having grown substantially. In other words the amount of shared information has greatly increased, helping those involved in this exchange to better understand each other. Better understanding will inevitably lead to:

- problem resolution

- better trust and confidence between the parties involved

- better knowledge and knowledge as to what may be possible.

Although the above may appear very simple it is a fact that the lack of simple communication between people is the single most important cause for all sorts of breakdowns/misunderstandings/missed opportunities/business failures. I cannot over stress the critical importance of achieving quality communication between people - of opening the windows and making the shared area as large as possible!

Without overstating the obvious, it was only by getting America, the EU, Russia and Iran to actually sit around a table and discuss the nuclear issue that some form of agreement could be negotiated that was acceptable to all parties involved. Joseph and Harry would have been elated!

So what is the relevance of all of this?

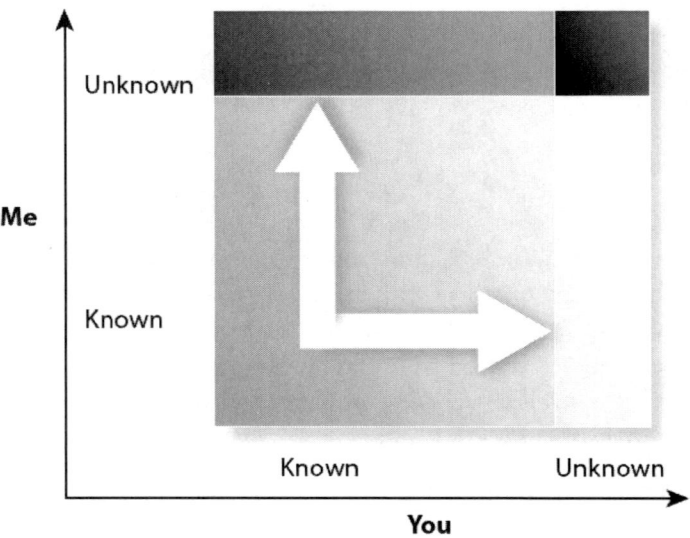

Johari's Window has direct and very real relevance in business, home life, one-to-one relationships and, as I have mentioned already, in politics both domestic and global.

Let's examine each in turn:

Business

"We need to have better communication" is a mantra from business, as is "people are our most important assets!"

Both of the above may be true, but the reality is that communication is often lacking and that people are rarely treated like assets and even more rarely actually treated like people! Johari's Window can have a direct impact on both without the need for either a massive investment of cash or huge organisational disruption. You will not need to bring in expensive consultants or engage in a so called 'Change Management Strategy'. What's required is a change in attitudes, a change in behaviour - both of which can be achieved by clear and simple leadership from the top.

Communication is essential to ensure that all employees within an organisation are treated with respect, as concerned and caring human beings, and not as assets of production that merely turn up to do what has to be done to secure their wage. The change in attitude of mind is absolutely critical. Consider the following:

- Why should all employees not be informed about the strategy and objectives of the business they work in?

- Why should all employees not be told the truth about the state of the business?

- Why should all employees' perceptions on what needs to be done better not be taken account of?

- Why should the Chairman and CEO of a business take seriously discussions with shareholders, plan institutional visits, plan AGMs, plan investor relations strategies and programmes, but not employee communications or employee visits?

- Why is it still considered to be a relative rarity for senior executives to walk the floor, visit their plant (offices, factories, shops, warehouses), take time to spend with their employees?

- Why is 'Management By Walking Around' (MBWA), not a standard part of every CEO's routine?

- Why is it so rare that senior management actively engages with their employees NOT for the purpose of negotiating terms and conditions, but to listen to, learn from and talk with the employees?

- Why is it so hard to ensure effective and trusted communication between employees and management, as evidenced by the recent spate of industrial disputes - for example, the industrial disputes suffered by BA in both 2009 and 2010?

- Why was the 'Ask Archie' initiative thought to have been so revolutionary when Archie Norman placed that button on his lapel as CEO of ASDA that eventually led to the supermarket's successful turnaround?

- Why does it take a TV programme 'Undercover Boss' to uncover what employees really think about their management?

Here are noteworthy examples of both a negative and a positive:

> **Negative:** *Financial Times* December 19th 2009, "it was either this or McDonalds" (Flinch, FT Interview with Michael O'Leary, chief executive of Ryanair). In the interview Michael O'Leary, CEO of Ryanair, expresses his view on MBAs and management consultants, and then says, "My staff are my most important asset. Bullshit! Staff is usually your biggest cost!" No great surprise then that employee survey after employee survey highlights the general level of dissatisfaction with the quality of

internal/employee communications. Mr O'Leary may have a successful business in that passengers want his low cost air-travel offer and employees may be prepared to put up with his approach to business - but if push came to shove there simply would not be staff loyalty and support to come to his rescue. Interestingly, by late 2013 it became clear that Ryanair's main competitor, easyJet, had made significant competitive gains, had become much more profitable and was growing much faster as they were pursuing a policy of much more inclusive treatment of staff and passengers. Under Carolyn McCall's leadership easyJet has clearly taken on-board the need for much more open communications and is, as a consequence, delivering much better service to its passengers.

Positive: Ricardo Semler's book *'Maverick!'* (Tabletun Inc., 1993) outlines how a relatively small Brazilian manufacturer became one of Brazil's leading industrial concerns by implementing a series of changes essentially aimed at involving and communicating with the workforce. Whilst a massive simplification of Semler's achievements, the essence is the democratisation of employees. The book is an excellent read, and really makes one think and question. Similarly, looking at the companies at the top of 'Best Place to Work' league tables *(The Sunday Times Best 100 Companies to Work For/Fortune 100 - Great Place to Work)*, engagement and empowerment are nearly always made reference to, neither of which would be possible without effective communication.

In business, Johari's Window can and should be applied both formally in performance reviews and informally by creating as open an environment as possible.

When I was CEO of Valin Pollen, and when I chaired TACK International, Coffee Point Plc, and CVO Group, I made a deliberate and conscious effort to engage not only with my board colleagues and the immediate executive teams, but also with as wide a group of employees as possible. I held sandwich lunches with a cross section of randomly selected employees to be able to have informal and genuinely open discussions. Usually they would start with silence! No one being sure what to say, how open they should be, whether the lunch was on the record or off the record? I would then start by telling them about myself - giving them some background about my own career, including some more personal stuff about likes and dislikes, family and non-work related activities – and, amazingly, that helped to break the ice and get some dialogue going. In other words opening a few 'windows' on me triggered others to do likewise. I would also lay down the ground rules, i.e. everything said was totally off the record!

It seems to me, based on many such experiences, that the vast majority of people are perfectly prepared to engage in relatively open discussion if they feel that openness is a two-way street. Hence by being prepared to provide details about myself that was not in the open domain, others were prepared to relax and partake more openly themselves. Just a few weeks ago this is exactly what happened with one of the companies I chair and when for the first time I met with all the non-board employees - a very real practical example of Joahari's Window facilitating communication.

Not surprisingly, on numerous occasions these lunches produced some terrific ideas that were absolutely relevant to the business, ideas that were easy to implement and frequently ideas that reached across silos, departments, sections and business units on the basis that the lunch was one of the first opportunities for people in different parts of the business to talk to each other - a genuine example of 'windows' being opened and the shared space being enlarged. This is real, this has happened on a number of occasions.

I also have experience of founder/CEO's resistance to such open meetings. "What a total waste of time and money", I recall being thrown at me. "You are seriously out of your mind if you think I am going to be supportive of you engaging with employees, they might think they have a role to play beyond what they are hired for and that would be disastrous!" I was aggressively lectured but, having persevered, an initial gathering took place and the participants found it thrilling and hugely motivating. None of the participants felt in any way that they should have greater involvement in decision making; they were just delighted to have been consulted, listened to and involved - for the first time!

Equally, making time to spend with the workforce, employees and staff of your business is important, and is part of 'opening windows'. Being accessible is the key. If you live in an office, rarely step outside, make everyone always come to you and never bother to engage with those who are working for you, you are essentially not only ensuring that your window is firmly closed, but that it is perceived to have the shutters down too. Not particularly encouraging or motivating to others. What is tragic is that getting out of the office for the odd day is not difficult, not expensive, and certainly not complicated to arrange. All it takes is a tiny bit of planning and the WILL to do it. As I repeated time and again in my earlier book: 'Do it, do it now'.

Again, this is something I did and still do frequently but irregularly, both in my executive and non-executive capacities. At times it was just a valuable learning opportunity for me to be able to have direct feedback from employees, to be able to listen to what employees had to say. At times there were valuable insights gained that I took back and either acted on or reviewed with the executive team. For example, in one situation a driver asked why we didn't have smaller vans given that in his experience he was driving his van three quarters full. A simple question based on direct experience. As some vans came to be renewed that is exactly what we did, saving both upfront and lease cost and, importantly, operational cost too as smaller vans were cheaper to run. This is a small example of the shared space being enlarged to the benefit of the business. Many such small examples can accumulate and have a fairly significant impact.

I am absolutely of the opinion that creating real engagement with one's employees; creating real opportunities for dialogue; ensuring that the windows are not only open, but are known by all to be open, has substantial benefits to the business. Benefits that can be totally disproportional with occasionally significant bottom-line results including the less obvious benefits of employee retention, lower staff turnover, better informed and motivated employees and better overall atmosphere for all to work in. What's totally crazy is that this can be achieved with virtually no investment of cash, just some limited senior executive time and a preparedness to act.

What could be easier?

Home

Johari's Window has direct and very real relevance in the home too. As this is a short book aimed at the business community I shall not dwell on this to any significant extent, apart from making a number of small observations:

- Lack of open communication between partners is probably one of the key reasons for the breakdown of relationships.

- Creating an open environment in which everyone in the 'family unit' feels able and happy to be included is not only positive for the adults but has a strong positive impact on the children, and can have a beneficial educational impact on them as well.

- Couples being prepared to talk about their needs, likes and dislikes can substantially improve the quality of sexual relationships.

- The likelihood of serious issues such as drugs, crime, alcohol abuse, bullying etc. can be diminished in family units that encourage all members to talk openly about all issues - with nothing being classified as taboo or too difficult.

In March 2009, Bernard Madoff pleaded guilty to 11 federal felonies and admitted to turning his wealth management business into a massive Ponzi scheme that defrauded thousands of investors of billions of dollars (the amount missing from client accounts, including fabricated gains, was almost $65 billion). Without doubt this is the largest fraud in the world's history and yet none of his close work associates, his wife, nor his two sons who were working in the business are alleged to have known anything about it. He is now serving 150 years in a US prison. He was interviewed by the *Financial Times* (9th/10th April 2011, 'From behind bars, Madoff spins his story'), the article contained an amazing revelation: "In the end I was almost relieved. The pressure I was under in the last 16 years was almost unbearable. I wish they'd caught me sooner." Put another way, if he had been able to open Johari's Windows and talk to his wife and children he may have been able to stop the fraud long ago.

I have personally drawn this simple 2x2 on a pad and explained the core concept to people I have been close to and whom I thought could benefit from an understanding of the importance of enhanced communication. I have exchanged the principles of Johari's Window with therapist friends who have responded very favourably about the power of its simple logic and were somewhat surprised that they hadn't come across it in their own field.

One-to-one

Similarly on a one-to-one basis there are very real benefits that can be achieved by applying some of Johari's Window's simple principles - whether in the playground, in the home (as above), in any form of social gathering, committee, or organisational unit.

Wherever we interact with others on a one-to-one basis there could be benefits of opening the windows, perhaps just slightly to commence with and progressively thereafter. Clearly the extent and speed is dictated by circumstances and the degree to which the other party is prepared to reciprocate.

Politics

As I have already mentioned, the basic principles of Johari's Window is directly applicable to the most sensitive and most complex negotiations both in a domestic setting as well as, for example, negotiations between the various factions involved in Northern Ireland and globally whether it be the Israeli/Palestinian conflict; Syria's chemical weapons of mass destruction; or Iran's nuclear development programme! As the advertising campaign for BT once declared: "It's good to talk"!

Chapter 4
Product/Market Evaluations Matrix

For most businesses, irrespective of size, one of the recurring issues they confront is how best to develop their business. Which products to support? Which markets to seek to expand in? These are complex and often time consuming and expensive decisions, and this is exactly where our 2x2 matrix can come to the rescue. The matrix won't make the decision making any simpler, but provide a framework that can magnify the key issues that will need to be resolved and within which the implications of decisions can be assessed.

The Product/Market Evaluations matrix, a model that's been around for almost 50 years, was created by Igor Ansoff (December 12, 1918 – July 14, 2002, a Russian-American, applied mathematician and business manager, known as the father of strategic management) in 1965. It has since been applied by leading management consultancies as part of their toolkit, as well as put to practical use by many leading corporations.

So let us construct the matrix with MARKETS as axis y and PRODUCTS as axis x. Then let's sub-divide each into EXISTING MARKET and NEW MARKET; and EXISTING PRODUCT and NEW PRODUCT to create the matrix as follows:

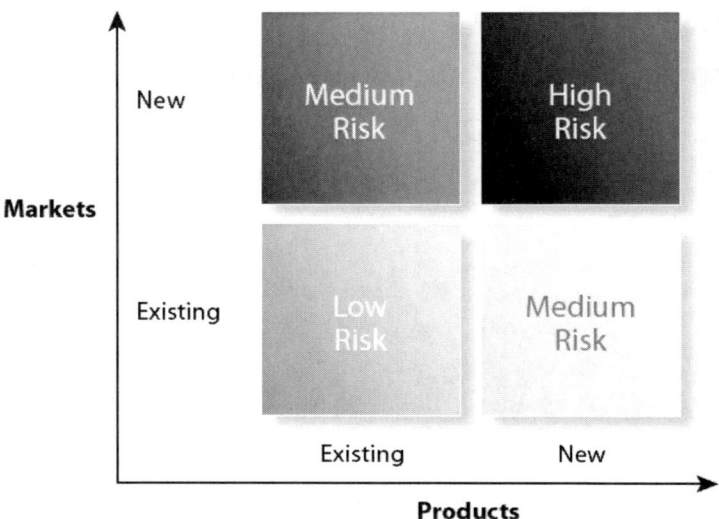

In the above matrix it is clear that the bottom left hand box rep-resented by the company's existing markets and existing products is a relatively low risk area. This is where the company is currently located. They should know their existing markets well and their competitive pressures. Within their existing markets they are supplying existing products, products that have already been proven and are acceptable to the market place. Products with a proven track record, a proven customer base, at an established price and with an existing distribution chan-nel. Whilst there are of course risks, these are largely known and manageable.

While no company should ever be complacent as competition can emerge from the most unexpected sources, this known/known product/market position is one of relative com-fort. Irrespective of comfort or perceived risks of this position it is critical to ensure thorough on-going market intelligence, vigilance about competition, and the closest of fingers on the pulse of consumers'/customers'/clients' needs and wants. We only need to think of non-sector competitors grabbing markets from well established operators in their known/known comfort zones - think of Swatch/easyJet/Dyson! Think of the prevailing demise of BlackBerry and Ericsson as the battle rages for domination in the smartphones market with Apple and Samsung as the current winners.

The critical importance of constant vigilance to ensure on-going monitoring and knowledge about customers' needs was dramatically introduced by the now famous 1960's article in Harvard Business Review by Theodore Levitt, 'Marketing Myopia':

> *"'Marketing Myopia' is the quintessential big hit HBR piece. In it, Theodore Levitt, who was then a lecturer in business administration at the Harvard Business School, introduced the famous question, "What business are you really in?" and with it the claim that, had railroad executives seen themselves as being in the transportation business rather than the railroad business, they would have continued to grow. The article is as much about strategy as it is about marketing, but it also introduced the most influential marketing idea of the past half-century: that businesses will do better in the end if they concentrate on meeting customers' needs rather than on selling products. 'Marketing Myopia' won the McKinsey Award in 1960."*

Therefore, however secure a position a company may be in - in its known market, with its known products - unless they are fully aware of their customers' needs they will be open to rapid demise by competitors that are. Within our evolving world dominated by technology, this need becomes ever greater. Consumers' needs are open to strong influence by other consumers' reviews posted on Facebook/ Twitter/ Flickr/ Tumblr/ YouTube, etc that can impact dramatically on a product's ability to continue to win and/or retain market share.

Moving to either a new market or a new product increases risk. A vast amount of work will be required to evaluate the attractiveness and suitability of either of these strategic steps. However, irrespective of how thorough an analysis and evaluation is undertaken, the fact is that there remain vast amounts of uncertainty.

Take for example very successful British companies that have expanded internationally, adding to their strong domestic market outlets in new international markets. Some very substantial organisations decided to enter what they perceived to be the largest market 'on their doorstep'. A market that spoke the same language, where there were more similarities with the UK than differences - that is the USA. Of course they undertook extensive market research. Of course they spent many hundreds of thousands of pounds doing detailed research and analyses. Many hired firms of management consultants to help them decide whether the market was suitable for entry and, if so, to evaluate and plan their market entry strategies. Companies of the size and reputation of Marks & Spencer and Midland Bank (before it was acquired by HSBC), took the plunge and, despite everything, lost vast fortunes of their shareholders' funds and ultimately pulled out, writing off the experience. Marks & Spencer acquired Brook Brothers and Midland acquired Croker Bank, both being divested at a later date.

Little wonder that the USA is often referred to as the 'graveyard' for British companies that sought overseas expansion. The story continues with Tesco pursuing an expansion strategy in California of its 'Fresh and Easy' stores as a test for further expansion in the USA. The results of Tesco's market entry strategy are questionable, with only 125 stores in Southern California, far short of the 500 anticipated by February 2010, with an expected loss of approximately $260m on an investment of $1.4billion! The ultimate conclusion of this venture was an embarrassing pull-out! As reported on by Gabi Thesing, September 10, 2013 8:55, Bloomberg:

> *"Tesco Plc (TSCO) agreed to sell most of its Fresh & Easy chain to billionaire Ron Burkle's Yucaipa investment company, allowing the UK grocer to exit the US after a failed six-year foray into the world's biggest economy.*

> *Fresh & Easy has never made a profit since it was built from scratch in 2007. Tesco has invested about 1 billion pounds ($1.6 billion) in the business in that period. Many analysts saw it as a drag on resources at a time when Tesco is struggling to maintain its dominant share of the U.K. grocery market.*

> *The sale to Yucaipa "represents the best outcome for Tesco shareholders and Fresh & Easy's stakeholders," Tesco Chief Executive Officer Philip Clarke said in a statement. "It offers us an orderly and efficient exit from the U.S. market."*

> *Tesco exited Japan last year and said August 9 it plans to merge its 131 stores in China with the country's second-biggest hypermarket chain, ending nearly a decade of independent operations in the country as sales decline."*

Clearly there are successes, some of which are highlighted below, including Sir Philip Green's Top Shop that recently-opened in New York to massive critical acclaim (but will it stand the test of time?).

It's not only British businesses expanding to the US that experience difficulties:

> *"Best Buy had huge plans to move into Europe and China. So far, it's failed in both markets — mainly because consumers don't like mega stores. It moved into the UK market in 2010 by buying a 50% stake in UK mobile phone company Carphone Warehouse and had planned to open 100 'Big Box' stores in the next few years. Analysts say that it failed in the UK because it announced its plans too early (two years ahead of time) and gave its competitors — primarily Dixons and Comet — a chance to respond. It also opened 'Big Box' stores, when Europeans prefer smaller shops. "It was the wrong format, at the wrong time, in the wrong market," Robert Gregory, research director at Planet Retail told the Guardian. It encountered similar problems in China. Last spring, it shut down nine of its stores in the region after being there for five years. Best Buy is also botching expansion plans in Turkey.*
>
> *Though the company determined its Europe plans before the recession hit — when things looked much differently, and the 'Big Box' concept was thriving in the U.S. — Best Buy should have considered a new strategy as it approached its launch dates (even if that meant delaying them again). The retailer was smart to partner with a UK company, but it could have gotten more feedback from its UK business partners before aggressively moving into the new market. According to Yahoo, "closing the 11 British stores would be the biggest admission of failure so far in the U.S. retailer's*

overseas expansion strategy". "

(Why Best Buy's Overseas Strategy Is Failing Aimee Groth, November 04, 2011 – *Business Insider*, War Room.)

The key point I am seeking to illustrate is the very real risk inherent in taking the decision to move into a new market, be that geographic, or a new market in terms of end customers, or channels of distribution. For example, just because you have enjoyed success as a developer of commercial property does not automatically mean that you will enjoy the same success in residential property. Or you may have been an outstanding wholesaler and find the transition into retail difficult and problematic.

Entering an existing market with a new product also has risks associated with it. The dynamics may be slightly different, consumer behaviour may be different, competitive pressures may be different – which all combine to escalate the degree of risk. When Coca-Cola decided to enter the UK market for bottled water they must have thought that they had undertaken sufficient research and, as a leading company already in the bottled drinks market, adding a new product would not be too demanding. However, after launching their new bottled water product, 'Dasani', Coca-Cola was forced into a high profile, embarrassing and expensive withdrawal after consumers' rejection of their product. Why? What had they got so very wrong? The fact was that UK consumers objected to paying a premium for a bottle of water, the origin of which was the same as that which came through their kitchen tap, but with 'purification'!

Was this not the same for British Airways when they decided to enter the UK market (an existing market) with their own low-cost, no frills (new product) offering, GO, in competition with what was then the emerging and rapidly growing market created by easyJet and Rynair? After just three years they decided to pull out selling GO initially to GO's management who subsequently sold to no other than easyJet!

How could two mega and hugely experienced companies such as Coca-Cola and British Airways have got it so wrong?

Tesco undertook yet another high risk venture with a move into a new product zone of retail banking, within their existing UK market. This, however, is likely to be a safer bet than the international expansion to the US as it is essentially offering another product/service to its very large and well-established UK customer base. A customer base that trusts the 'Tesco' brand and is hungry for new providers of banking services, hence the growth of Virgin Bank, Metro Bank and arch rival Sainsburys Bank!

Igor Ansoff's matrix highlights that moving from the safe and comfortable existing market/existing product situation to either a new market, or a new product, has significant risk implication.

These risk implications expand exponentially by moving to the fourth sector of entering a new market with a new product. As in all aspects of life there are of course some notable exceptions. Sir Richard Branson has been a serial developer of new businesses entering new markets with new products - Virgin Atlantic, Virgin Money, Virgin Music, Virgin Media and Virgin Trains are all examples of success but there have also been numerous failures - Virgin Wedding, Virgin Cosmetics/Perfumes and others that may not have even seen the light of day.

Sir Stelios Haji-Ioannou's easyGroup is similar in successfully building new markets with new products - easyJet, easyHotels, easyMoney, easyBus, easyInternet and, equally, has had numerous failures along the way including easyCinema.

The above are examples of entrepreneurs creating new businesses that by definition involve massive risks and can equally create massive returns if they work out. The notion of pushing into new markets with new products is very much focused on existing and well-established businesses that have identified new opportunities for their continued expansion. Perhaps one of the most successful serial new product/new market developers has been 3M, although the crown has to be given to Steve Jobs and Apple. The launch of the 'i' range of products from music to phone to touch-screen pads has been truly astonishing. As I said above, massive risks with massive returns - with Apple becoming the world's most valuable company by market capitalisation by August 2012.

In reality every time an entrepreneur creates a new business, this fourth section is being entered - a new market with a new product. It is a well-known statistical fact that out of every ten start-ups only two are likely to survive and only one is likely to achieve any degree of success. The toughness of entering new markets with new products does not put off real entrepreneurs who are convinced that they have got the right formula, they have got the right mix to establish a successful business - essentially they believe that they have created a 'better mouse-trap', and long may it be so.

Climbing Everest is fraught with danger. Over 200 people have died to date and yet more people are still signing-up to climb the mountain!

Yes, the risks are high, the matrix clearly demonstrates this. The decision as to whether to take the risk is that of the individual.

The matrix helps to illustrate the realities involved and define the situation. The rest is up to you.

Let us examine another situation. I have been involved with the recruitment/search sector in various capacities, as a practitioner and as chairman of a number of businesses. In my chairman's capacity I have come across situations in which management have created strategies that have involved taking their existing business from their current well-defined and well-known service/market sectors to new service market sectors. For example, a recruitment business that is operating successfully (say) in the UK, with a developed specialisation (say) in the retail sector, decides that it wishes to:

- expand internationally and

- wishes to move from retail into media as well.

You may think that making these two moves is not that significant, that the executive team will have thought through all the various issues and implications; will have fully assessed the associated risks; will have worked out how their existing business can support and be stretched to provide the launch for the proposed new developments, but the reality is often very different.

The executive team will of course have undertaken lots of related planning, but frequently the risks are just not fully explored. The risks are assumed to be relatively slight given the assumption that taking existing recruitment business from retail to media is a small incremental step requiring just a consultant with well established media credentials and moving an existing business from the UK to one other country is just opening another office, albeit in another country - but the risks are huge.

The diagram below demonstrates how the risk grows for the two proposed developments. Adding a new sector – media - means not only that the business will need to recruit a consultant with the established expertise in media, but will need to commence the development of both candidates and clients in the media sector virtually from scratch. They will need to establish a track record, a reputation and a proven capability to recruit in the sector. Moving from the UK to an international market, let's assume only across the channel to France, is much more than just opening a new office in the UK. Laws, regulations, established practices, are all different - even within the EU! The business will need to ensure that it has someone able to communicate fluently in the country's language (in this example French) to be able to deal with all the official regulations and requirements surrounding the establishment of a new office in a new country.

There will be associated currency risks of dealing not in pounds sterling but in euros. New bank accounts will be required and new tax jurisdictions will need to be considered. There will be the extended line of management to deal with too.

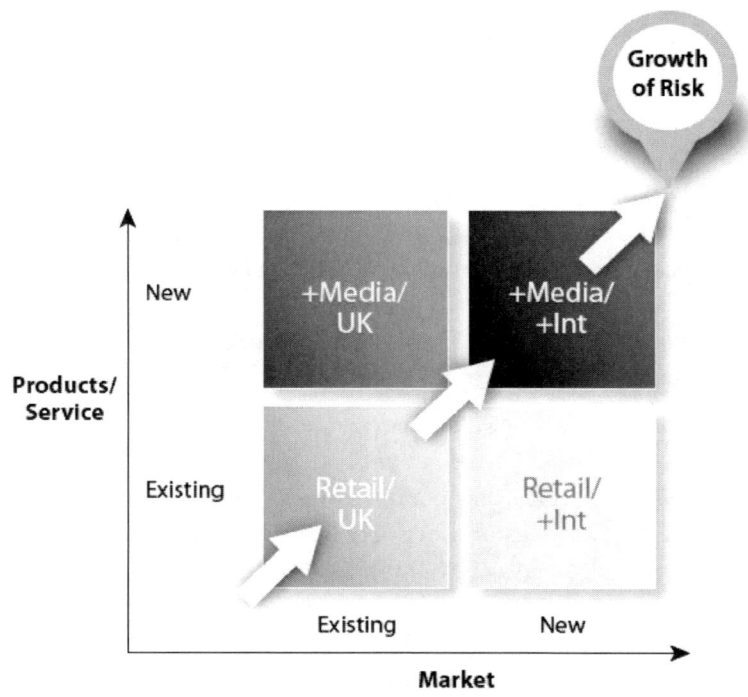

Taking both of the proposed moves together illustrates the magnitude of risk the business is taking on if it is to embark on both developments. Vastly more than may have been apparent to commence with. Vastly more than the business may be able to handle.

The above is based on real experience. One of the businesses that I was involved in undertook exactly the above - moving both into new service areas and new markets at the same time. I was appointed non-executive chairman when the wheels started to come off the vehicle, with severe problems being incurred: stretched cash-flow and a stretched management team, but unfortunately the damage had already been done. Unwinding such situations is complex, relatively lengthy and unfortunately both expensive and painful in terms of people!

The world's graveyard of business is jam-packed with businesses that have simply been unable to recover from the stress of over-expansion. Always well intentioned, always by executive teams that have achieved real success in their existing product/service and existing market domains, always by boards that have 'fully assessed the related risks' - one only needs to make reference to Royal Bank of Scotland's acquisition of ABN Amro and the resulting debacle to illustrate the point!

Businesses have come seriously undone because there was insufficient time allocated to considering the true implications (inherent in Igor Ansoff's product/market matrix) and the implied exponential growth in risk as the business undertakes actions which take it into the fourth 'new-new' square. Or is there just an overwhelming arrogance by boards and management teams that think they know better?

Moving on, the next chapter is focused on what is perhaps the most famous and the most widely used set of 2x2 boxes: SWOT analysis. SWOT analysis can be used on its own or as an integral part of both Igor Ansoff's product/market matrix or Johari's Window.

2X2 MANAGER

Chapter 5
SWOT Analysis

Here is another situational analysis technique, this time related to understanding your own business, or another business that you may be targeting for acquisition.

> "Albert S. Humphrey (1926 – 2005) an American business and management consultant who specialised in organizational management and cultural change is credited with the creation of the SWOT analysis technique while working for the Stanford Research Institute, now known as SRI International."

(Source: Wikipedia.)

SWOT stands for:

- Strengths
- Weaknesses,
- Opportunities and
- Threats

It is usually presented in a four-box format as per the below diagram. The difference from the previous 2x2 examples is that the axes applied can vary to whatever needs a situational review - from Market and Competition, to R&D and Manufacturing, People and Capital. The labels to each of the four boxes as portrayed below are the key thought drivers.

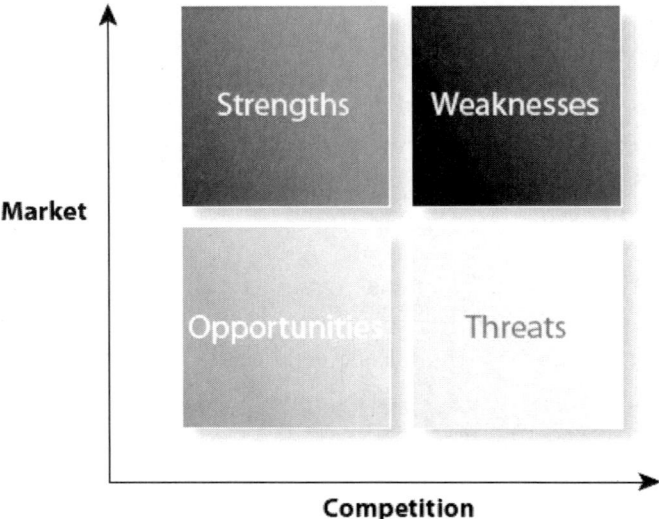

The thinking behind this simple device is to force management to articulate their understanding of the company's/business' situation. In the example above this would be in terms of Market and Competition. The questions that could be asked would be along the following lines:

- What are the definable, measurable and non-measurable strengths of my business in terms of the markets we operate in?

  For example, our market share places us as the number two player in the market. We therefore have strong market share, but is our market share growing or declining? Have we won or lost market share over the past year? We have a position of strength as the number two player, but is this defendable? For example Nokia was the leading manufacturer and distributor of mobile phones in the world. They had the largest market share of new phone sales (and even today they probably have the largest installed base of users) but over the past few years they have been losing market share to the newer 'smartphones' such as Samsung's Galaxy, iPhone and (originally) BlackBerry. They seem to have woken up to the realities of the market and their competitive positioning too late resulting in their 'fire sale' to Microsoft. Similarly, Research in Motion Limited, the Canadian owner of BlackBerry devices is seeing its market share dramatically attacked by the iPhone so successfully created and launched by Apple. It is now questionable whether Blackberry will be able to remain as an independent business, or whether it too will be purchased/rescued by a competitor. Perhaps the most famous for being number two in the market was the car rental company, AVIS, who's marketing campaign was directly based on that fact – "AVIS we try harder" - i.e actually creating a strategic advantage from being number two!

• What are the definable, measurable and non-measurable weaknesses of my business in terms of the markets we operate in?

Although we are number two, the leader has clear dominance and real price advantages that we are unable to bridge for the time being. Again referring to Nokia in the mobile phone market it became clear that they lost ground to the technology inherent in smartphones developed initially by Research in Motion then substantially changed by Apple, and subsequently grabbed by other global players such as Samsung. The ex-Microsoft senior executive propelled into Nokia as CEO, Stephen Elop, reached out to his old company and established a formal collaboration aimed at rapidly bridging the identified weakness - but even this failed to stop the ever more rapid decline. As Mr Elop commented in February 2011: "The first iPhone was shipped in 2007 and we still don't have a product that is close to their experience. Android came on the scene just over two years ago and this week they took our leadership position in smartphone volumes. Unbelievable."

In the growing world of search engines Google is clearly the dominant player. So other global competitors need to find ways to evaluate their positions of relative strengths and weaknesses and find ways to compete with Google - as was clearly demonstrated in the following headline in the Financial Times of 23rd August 2012: "Baidu to challenge Goggle on travel info" (Baidu being China's largest search engine company by market share). In the world of on-line shopping one would believe that Amazon is a clear global leader when in effect it is China's Alibaba.

- What are the definable, measurable and non-measurable opportunities of my business in terms of the markets we operate in?

For the mobile phone market, despite the extraordinary growth that has been experienced over the past decade, there continues to be massive opportunities - especially as the so called BRIC markets (Brazil, Russia, India and China) continue to grow and their populations' disposable income expands. Within Africa mobile phones are facilitating contact and communications without the massive infrastructure that was required by the fixed line telecommunications of the past. Mobile communications are in turn opening up access to computing and, in particular, the extraordinary powers of the internet. It is today not impossible for there to be internet access in a village hundreds of miles in the wilderness - without fixed line telecoms connections.

Mobile operators are increasingly recognising the virtually unlimited possibilities that their smartphone devises may be able to deliver from mobile money, to security - opportunities that may only be limited by the market's ability to adjust and adapt. This was fabulously exploited by Dr Mohamed 'Mo' Ibrahim, a Sudanese-British mobile communications entrepreneur and billionaire. He worked for several other telecommunications companies before founding Celtel, which when sold for $3.4 billion had over 24 million mobile phone subscribers in 14 African countries. Mo saw an opportunity and created a business other much better and longer established mobile phone operators failed to see! Others have also failed to see how mobile phones can create new ways of doing old transactions such as banking:

> *"At least in the realm of cashless marketplaces, the east African country has been thundering along the cutting edge since the 2007 launch of M-Pesa—the M is for "mobile"; pesa is Swahili for "money."*
>
> *What was originally conceived as an efficient method*

to make payments on microloans has been rapidly adopted by Kenyans as a way to send money from urban centers back to rural hometowns."

Published Monday, 11 Nov 2013, 7:00 AM ET by Matt Twomey, Special to CNBC.com

- What are the definable, measurable and non-measurable threats of my business in terms of the markets we operate in?

Although we are number two with a strong market share, are there new market entrants with strong corporate or private equity backing? What are the barriers to entry, and how defensible are they? Certainly no-one would have imagined just a few years ago that Google would be a player in the mobile phone market via its Android operating system. It is arguable that the launch of smartphones created a new market, a market that the traditional mobile phones were not in. It is possible to argue that the introduction of the 'tablet' initiated by Apple with their hugely successful iPad, created yet another market. Unimaginable a few years ago this is a market that by 2013 had grown at the fastest rate of any new device. Who would have thought that the originator of smartphones, BlackBerry, would be outmanoeuvred by Apple's iPhone and other android competitors, to the extent of virtually putting BlackBerry out of business?

Mapping out the threats that exist and may exist requires not only in depth knowledge of the market, but also a willingness to admit that change is a constant. Knowing the market in depth requires knowledge not only of numbers (size, share, value etc) but also of needs, wants and perceptions of consumers. Avoiding marketing myopia is critical.

Avoiding the arrogance that comes from huge success is critical.

As the markets have shown time and time again no company, however successful, however enormous, however outstanding at what it did, can assume it may not be threatened by both new and existing competitors. Marketing myopia is a killer of giants!

• What are the definable, measurable and non-measurable competitive strengths of my business?

Even in the hugely difficult competitive markets of 2014 BlackBerry's massive installed base is a major competitive strength. BlackBerry achieved this massive market penetration because theirs was the first smartphone in the market - they were both reliable and were perceived to be the easiest to use. If they can overcome having been left behind in the smartphone market by a newer generation and bring to market technologically advanced, reliable and easy to use tablets and smartphones, they may be able to retain and convert existing users and even win back past users who have moved across to competitors. A hugely tough scenario for BlackBerry to execute and one that the stock markets have largely discounted - but not totally impossible!

BMW's acquisition of the 'Mini' brand, along with other assets, have served it well. BMW recognised that there is potentially something special about the 'Mini' brand offering clear competitive strengths as long as they were able to create a vehicle that was suitable for the badge. They did just that. They have built a hugely successful 'Mini' range of contemporary vehicles that have taken market share and delivered huge financial success. This is the very same success that was created by FIAT for its re-launch of their totally modernised Fiat 500, which became Europe's largest selling small vehicle.

Working out your business competitive strengths is a complex process that needs to take account of every dimension of the business. It needs a highly granulated analysis and above all a sense of total honesty and a recognition that just because something worked in the past is no guarantee that it will work again in the future. To stick with the motor industry - simply re-branding was not sufficient when British Leyland tried to re-introduce an up-market brand, Rover. It failed miserably. It essentially stuck a 'Rover' brand on a substandard vehicle and was surprised that the product failed to sell! Especially so as the market was changing and Rover's competitors were rapidly becoming much more sophisticated – think of BMW, Mercedes and Audi! British Leyland failed to work out in any sort of detail the measurable and non-measurable competitive strengths of their business.

- What are the definable, measurable and non-measurable opportunities my business may have in relation to my competitors?

In the massively competitive world of jet engines Rolls-Royce created a reputation for excellence for its Trent series, but the competitive world is ever moving and highly dynamic. To create a defensible position Rolls-Royce introduced 'TotalCare' as part of its competitive offer (i.e. an on-going support and maintenance programme for its engines on a global basis). This has been highly successful and now accounts for a significant part of the company's overall profitability.

By introducing allocated seating easyJet provided customers with something they greatly appreciated and valued, leading to growing market share in the massively competitive low-cost airlines sector and, importantly, taking a strong lead over their arch competitor, Ryanair. Easyjet also delivered increased profitability given their growing load factor/ utilisation which enabled them to pay higher dividends to their shareholders - so an all round win-win!

• What are the definable, measurable and non-measurable competitive weaknesses of my business?

Are book retailing, music retailing and card retailing destined to extinction as on-line alternative delivery method-ologies and pricing structures are destroying the economics of bricks and mortar retailing?

Given the identifiable competitive weaknesses, are there steps that can be taken to rectify and recover? The large UK based book and music retailer, HMV, is undergoing sub-stantial strategic shift in order to use its competitive strength - presence in the high street - in a way that will restore profitability even if it means moving away from its traditional core products. But only time will tell whether it is able to adjust sufficiently to the inherent weaknesses of being a retailer in a market that has shifted essentially on-line.

Similarly, to what extent can traditional travel agents sur-vive? Thomas Cook had a near death event a number of years ago and under the leadership of a new CEO, Harriet Green, they have come out fighting. (Harriet Green was named Veuve Cliquot Business Women of the Year for her transformation of the beleaguered travel operator.) With re-positioning, re-engineered offers and a much improved operating platform they have survived. Sustainability given the unrelenting pressures from on-line remains to be seen, but the stock-markets have reacted very favourably.

- What are the definable, measurable and non-measurable threats my business may be facing related to my competitors?

  If a market is attractive and continuing to grow more and more competitors will be attracted to enter that market, some from very low cost countries. This can lead to commoditisation of what may have been perceived earlier as a market with well-established and defendable brands. Is this not happening already with the growth of highly attractive and competitive 'smartphones' and 'tablets' from own label retailers such as Aldi and Tesco?

The above may seem to be a relatively easy exercise, but it is anything but! If this analysis is to be undertaken seriously, it takes a great deal of detailed analytical input, thorough evaluation of the market, thorough understanding of all the competitors, the business' own performance, financial, operational and whatever other metrics may be appropriate, including human resources and, of course, the customers and their wants and needs.

SWOT analysis can be immensely helpful when considering the acquisition of another company. Rather than holding the mirror up to your own business, use the 4 boxes to gain as deep an understanding of the business of the company being targeted. Do the analysis, do the research, do the evaluation to dig as deeply as possible to understand as much as possible.

Not everything can or should be analysed purely in financial terms. Not everything can be inputted into a financial model. The target company's strengths and weaknesses, their threats and their opportunities are important to gain a true picture. This sort of analysis can have a material bearing on the ultimate valuation. I have known this sort of SWOT analysis providing the ammunition to facilitate the indicative price being chipped effectively, or the contrary: the analysis substantiating the strong and defensible competitive position justifying the premium pricing.

A business that has a number of operating divisions, or a number of subsidiaries can use SWOT analysis on each discrete business. SWOT is not just for the parent company.

This approach may seem fairly basic but one of the most profound questions asked around the board table is "What business are we in?" This was one of the penetrating questions Peter Drucker (1909-2005), often referred to as the man who invented management (Business Week, November 2005), used to ask of managers at the companies he visited. "What business are we in?" is a typical 'idiots question' yet one with the most awesome power. For example, the CEO of Black and Decker once said: "People don't go into a DIY store because they need one of our drills. They go because they need a hole in the wall." Wonderbra in their internal communications to staff once said: "We do not sell underwear. We do not sell lingerie. What we sell is self-confidence for women." Equally it has been suggested that Harley Davidson does not sell motorbikes, they sell the concept of freedom to middle-aged men.

To be able to answer "What business are we in?" in a credible manner requires a thorough understanding of your market and your competition, how you are doing within your market and how you are doing competitively. That is exactly what this 2x2 is all about, and it is why SWOT analysis is known and used globally by all types of organisations, in all types of sectors. That is why SWOT is taught at business schools and employed as part of their tool kit by management consultants. That is why you will come across it in the boardroom and on the shop floor. SWOT analysis is truly a universal tool.

In addition it is occasionally thought to be a good idea to apply the same sort of thinking to the prevailing management itself. In other words:

"How are we doing?"

"What are our strengths and weaknesses, individually and as a group?"

Some may consider this challenging. It is! It takes a relatively confident board and management to be willing to open up.

For larger quoted companies undertaking such a review at board level is no longer just a random occurrence led by a for-ward thinking chairman. Corporate governance is increasingly requiring boards to undertake performance reviews on an annual basis, but there continues to be confusion and discom-fort as to how best to achieve the desired objective. Self-review; review by the chairman; external review by a specialist firm; external review by specialist board review sections of search firms; etc?

For me bringing in external assessors/board evaluators seems inappropriate in some circumstances. Bringing in a search firm's specialist board appraisal unit I find totally unacceptable - the equivalent of foxes in chicken huts. I do not accept the notion of 'Chinese walls' and simply do not believe either that search firms have sufficiently professional specialist consultants available, nor that the information that they gather in the pro-cess would remain sufficiently confidential. The insights they may obtain could be too appetising for them not to wish to use at a future date!

My preferred solution is 'self-help'. In reality if a board has an effective non-executive chairman together with a seasoned senior independent director (SID), it should be able to create and implement an assessment process for itself. This takes trust and a high degree of openness. Clearly this is not always possible, but if there is a well functioning board with good and open interaction at board level the chances are high that this could work.

If, however, there are deep divisions, abusive/dominant personalities, non-communicative directors or a lack of trust and respect, then going external is absolutely the right thing to do. If you choose this option go to an independent and specialist boards evaluation firm NOT associated with a search firm, or any other consultancy. Specialisation is really important in this area.

I have done both of the above - in one case undertaking the assessment by entrusting a non-executive to lead an agreed process; and in another by bringing in an external expert. The results were positive is both cases in the sense that they both identified specific actions required to be taken by the board, and the Chairman had the strengths to ensure that implementation was effectively undertaken. This is key! Undertaking the assessment is just the first step - ensuring acceptance and then implementation is vital. If there is not a commitment to implement, don't waste the time or the money on this type of an exercise.

So reverting to the core premise of undertaking a board review - of utilising SWOT analysis as part of the basic evaluation process - if done well, can result in excellent insights and improvements, especially when linked to the management team applying Johari's Window (see chapter 3) to ensure there is effective and open communication between all the team members.

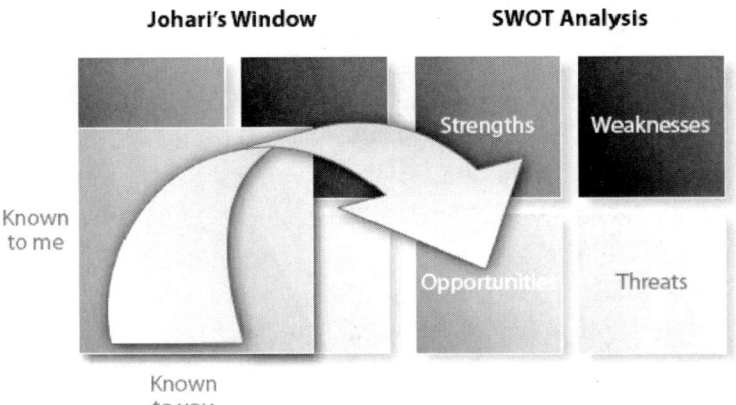

Johari's Window   **SWOT Analysis**

Known to me

Known to you

Strengths   Weaknesses

Opportunities   Threats

By applying Johari's Window to substantially increase the size of the shared knowledge box, by gaining commitment from all around the table to be openly and constructively critical, to share perceptions and knowledge, will help to undertake the SWOT analysis by directly feeding information across in terms of relative perceived strengths and weaknesses.

Applying both SWOT and Johari's Window in a rigorous way could provide all the evaluation required in a relatively easy and effective manner. Why this is not undertaken more frequently is a mystery to me.

Not only appropriate for board evaluation, SWOT analysis can be an effective component part of evaluating staff. Knowing your people, their strengths and weaknesses is vital for all businesses - this should not be a 'nice to have', this should be a 'must have'.

So, let me finish this chapter by providing a simple illustration of how SWOT may be used with different axes.

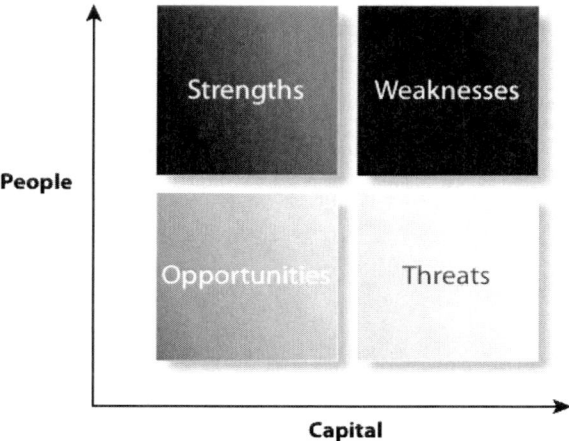

How are we doing in terms of developing our people, in terms of having the right people in the right roles, in ensuring we have succession planning, in terms of rewarding our people? How efficiently are we utilising the capital within the business? Do we have sufficient working capital and are we sufficiently capitalised, or are we over weighed with debt?

This type of analysis can lead to a detailed strategic review of the business and the various component parts within the business. Which units are generating cash and which are consuming cash?

So, from the relatively simple, let's move next to the fairly complex, yet still a 2x2 matrix. We shall next consider the methodology created by Boston Consulting Group to evaluate portfolio investments. These are logical next steps to be able to continue the analysis created by the above.

Chapter 6
Boston Consulting Group's Growth-Share Matrix

The Growth-Share Matrix was developed by Bruce Henderson of the Boston Consulting Group in the early 1970s. The prime objective was to be able to illustrate the important relationship between market growth and market share as it relates to the various units within an organisation, hence the title for this matrix, 'Growth-Share'.

The key conclusion reached was that units are typically at varying stages within a portfolio. Units may be growing at different speeds and may be at different stages in their life cycle. As a consequence they may require to be managed in different strategic ways. 'One size' strategic thinking does not fit all, hence it is important to know what stage in their life cycle various units have reached.

Bruce Henderson and the Boston Consulting Group developed this matrix in combination with another of their innovations called the 'Learning Curve'. (The learning curve expresses the relationship between experience and efficiency: as an individual or organization gets more experienced at a task, he/she/it will usually become more efficient.) The Growth-Share Matrix visually illustrates that increase in relative market share results in increased cash generation, mainly due to greater efficiencies from moving along the learning curve; and that rapidly growing businesses, businesses that were growing their market penetration, were requiring increased investment in assets and productive capacity and hence were consuming cash.

The above evaluation of the stages of development of a business, division, subsidiary, or an investment within a portfolio of investments can be achieved through the application of, amongst other analytical approaches, the SWOT analysis described in chapter 5.

It therefore follows that the location of a business unit in the Growth-Share Matrix is an indication of its ability either to generate or consume cash, grow and expand market share or decline (see below):

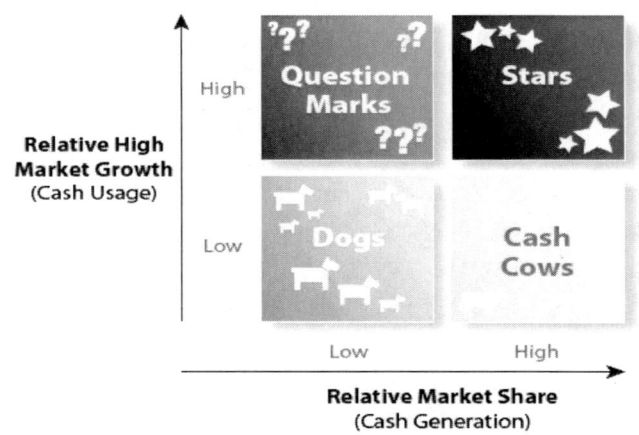

Market growth serves as a proxy for industry attractiveness, and relative market share serves as a proxy for competitive advantage. In other words the faster an identifiable industrial segment is seen to be growing the more attractive it is said to be. For example, it is clear in the world today that the 'tablet' market is continuing along a rapid growth trajectory, hence bringing in new players and new product variations. Within this 'tablets' market it is also clear that Apple's iPad is the winner in terms of market share - which Apple seems able to continue to grow, without decreasing the price of its product.

The Growth-Share Matrix, as shown above, thus maps the business units' position within these two important determinants of profitability. It is as a consequence of this categorisation that four specific symbolic positions have been created that business units can find themselves in as follows: CASH COW, STAR, DOG and QUESTION MARK.

Each one of these I shall now explore in greater detail.

CASH COW - this is typically a business that has reached a relatively mature stage in its development within a relatively mature market of which it has a good share.

With a strong competitive position, it is able to hold its pricing and generates reliable and growing positive cash flows.

The BCG model suggests that business units of this nature are prime to be 'milked' for profit and cash, thereby generating the funding required for investment into the stars of the future.

Unless there are massively unpredicted shifts in the market, or major discontinuities, cash cows should be able to go on generating reliable cash flows for a good number of years supporting not only investment into stars but also more basic research and development activity, funding for sorting out whether question marks have profitable futures and for other cash rich needs such as dividend policy and administrative requirements. For example, within pharmaceutical companies it is well known that they apply this thinking to their range of drugs. Once a drug has gone through the massively expensive process of R&D, through clinical trials, and has been accepted within the medical and pharmacological communities, it is likely to enjoy a period of high growth protected by patents, limiting competition, so it will also be able to enjoy high prices. Once the patent period has been exhausted, the drug will still command significant market share, at a relative premium to the white labelled 'commodity' drugs, thereby generating significant cash flows for its parent company. The brand 'Nurofen' is a great example, now very much a cash cow in a commoditised market full of similar products with the ibuprofen ingredient.

Within the fast moving consumer goods sector there are numerous examples of well-established products that are essentially cash cows for their owners. They have been around for decades and apart from the odd small change in packaging are identical in every other way. Marmite, Hovis, Corn Flakes and Coca-Cola are just four long standing products. They all have their imitators; they can all be obtained in an 'own label' format; yet they continue to have a loyal following, and often continue to enjoy premium pricing.

The technology sector is full of various product versions that have moved into the cash cow category as their newer versions take off and storm the market. The newer versions being bought by those who always want cutting edge products and are willing to pay the premium; whilst the 'just older' version is bought by an ever increasing number of followers who appreciate the slightly reduced price and 'proven' technology. The iPhone comes to mind with the current version to be superseded by the next iteration - and yet managing to create excitement and lengthy queues for the latest version.

It is however, important that there is no misunderstanding. Cash cows do need on-going investment if they are to continue to deliver benefit to their owners. They need to be relevant to the times, they need to be tweaked in terms of packaging and presentation. They need on-going advertising and marketing support. What they don't need is the level of investment of a star, nor the level of focus and support. They are well established, with a well-defined market presence and positioning.

STAR - these are the statistically few, the one in ten, the bet that paid off!

These are the star performers that have phenomenal growth trajectories, are rapidly winning market share and rapidly moving into both profit and cash positive territory. But these stars also require significant on-going funding to ensure they continue to grow and secure more market share, and retain their competitive advantage. Apple's iPhone and iPad are excellent examples, as was Facebook as it rapidly continued to grow its unique users past 100 million, 300 million, 500 million, 800 million and on. But the most extraordinary star of 2013 was Twitter, seeing its market penetration grow rapidly, resulting in a massive valuation during its initial public offering (IPO) in November 2013. "The $26 per-share pricing gives the company – which has not made a profit for the last three years – a value of $14.2bn - an extraordinary achievement however one looks at it!"

In the more traditional world of engineering it may be possible to suggest that the revival of Jaguar Land Rover Limited, under its Indian ownership, has created stars out of both the Jaguar and the Land Rover brands, with both vehicle ranges reaching levels of sales never seen before on a global basis. From what were once perceived as dogs and potentially cash cows, investment, design, technology, engineering and great market positioning have created outright stars.

Perhaps the best-known British entrepreneur/inventor is Sir James Dyson. Sir James is a British industrial designer and founder of the Dyson company. He is the inventor of the Dual

Cyclone bagless vacuum cleaner, which works on the principle of cyclonic separation, named as Dyson Vacuum Cleaner; with a number of other innovative products such as Dyson Air Multiplier™ fans and Dyson AirBlade Hand Dryer. All of these products took untold years to develop and commercialise. Only Sir James knows the number of rejected products along the journey. But the winners have been spectacular, enjoying global success and creating significant financial returns, until their IP runs out and imitations are brought to the market.

Both academics and consultants would argue that ideally every well diversified portfolio should always have stars that will become the next cash cows and ensure future cash generation. Sometimes easier said than done! Certainly all large portfolio investors, including VC (venture capital) and PE (private equity) investors would strive for this to be the case.

It is important to stress that stars can be reborn. A product that may have seemed to have matured and faded can be resuscitated. The classic footwear of the '60s, Hush Puppies, were fashion stars and then faded and were on the verge of oblivion when they were reborn into a star category. This was largely through adoption by college students in the US. Marmite is unquestionably a mature long established product with a strong market share. In all respects Marmite is a cash cow except that a whole suite of new products have been launched all based on Marmite's strong market recognition and positioning. These new products are much more like stars than cash cows. They require significant investment and have yet to create dominant market positions.

Some years ago Rolls-Royce's Trent engines were stars. The Trent engine series is now probably closer to a cash cow, although there may well be newer versions that are still very much drawing large amounts of investment and are characteristic of stars. Certainly Rolls-Royce's large installed base of Trent engines with airlines around the world is a source of excellent on-going cash flow through their support and maintenance contracts characteristic of cash cows.

The world of fashion is hugely exposed to rapidly rising stars and equally rapid falling off - often into extinction. Who can explain the emergence of Crocs, Ugg boots and the rise and fall of certain fashion houses. Take, for example, the quintessentially British house of Burberry that has been revitalised and taken to a level of international standing by its then CEO, Angela Ahrendt. This was unheard of in its long history since it was established in 1856! It was an unqualified global success, a genuine star. Whereas some stars of the '60s - Mary Quant, BIBA - have faded over the decades and not been seen since.

Within the world of professional services there can also be star performers. They can emerge over years of investment, development and steady growth, and reach a tipping point that accelerates them to global stardom. Often these firms are built on reputation and professional excellence. McKinsey is perhaps a name with global resonance. A clear star, McKinsey can attract the best talent and the best clients and is able to consistently maintain its premium pricing. Within the world of accountancy, Arthur Andersen was in a similar position, until its reputation got blown almost overnight by the collapse of Enron and the ensuing whirlwind accusations of faulty and corrupt business practices. This instantly destroyed Arthur Andersen's reputation and its ability to sustain its business model. The star that took decades to build burnt in a nanosecond! (But not totally. Many of Andersen's performing parts were acquired - the most notable being their whole UK practice - acquired by Deloitte, which over time helped to propel Deloitte into a leading position itself!)

The point of this is to illustrate that this is neither a one off characterisation nor simple.

Stars can and do fade, at times very fast. Boo.com was a star dot.com initiative a decade ago and failed rapidly; similarly with MySpace purchased by News International for a vast amount and dumped for a fraction of what they paid a few years later. Facebook was clearly a star well into 2013 - but will it be able to maintain its positioning or start to fade? Instagram and Tumblr are both on their way up but will they face new competition in the future that will halt their progress?

Will electric cars be the stars to come or, given the huge discovery of traditional sources of energy via hydraulic fracturing 'fracking' (which itself is in a star stage of development), make what was seen as an urgent need for green cars fade?

DOG - at the other extreme are the investments which have declined, have gone past their prime, are losing market share and are in low growth and/or declining markets, but are continuing to consume working capital, with very little or no return.

These are highly unattractive investments, or business units, and decisive action is usually required to eject them from a portfolio or company. They may however, be able to survive in different environments, and hence are frequent candidates for management buy-outs. For example, in the late '80s Redland PLC (of roof tiles fame) disposed of its division consisting of plastic pipes and bathroom fittings. The business was acquired through a management buy-in/buy-out (BIMBO), renamed Caradon Plc, which then became one of the stock-exchange's success stories of the early '90s!

As already mentioned, both the Rover and Jaguar car brands and production facilities are examples of dogs that have gone on to survive under different ownership. Both have been purchased by an Indian conglomerate that believe that they will be able to apply lower manufacturing costs to continue to produce brands that have well-established global awareness. The success is clear for all to see with both brands enjoying significant global acclaim and achieving record levels of sales.

Dogs are tough for boards to deal with. They are usually well-known and often well loved businesses that have been around for a very long time. They are exposed to the classic risk of 'putting new money after bad' - in other words boards not being alert to the terminal decline of an old and loved business unit and trying to invest to help it recover. There is also sentimental attachment. As I referenced in my previous book (*It's the People! What really drives great management and leadership,* 2010, LID Publishing) this type of investment decision requires the 'positive no'. No, this is not an investment that should be authorised. No, the unit is in terminal decline and should either be closed down or it should be ensured that no more funds or management time is required to be invested; or it should be disposed of to another owner; or a management buy-out should be facilitated. The bottom line is that this is not a business that should be retained.

Book retailers around the world are struggling with exactly this type of decision. The printed book, loved by many, has been exposed to massive discontinuity via electronic publishing. The electronic book, or e-book, is fast and easy to obtain/purchase by simply downloading, much cheaper to purchase, and easier to carry and use via the increasingly wide range of e-readers, the most significant being Amazon's Kindle. So, for how long can chains of book shops such as Barnes and Noble in the US continue? As of October 2013 Barnes and Noble still had over

670 stores in the US, but its on-line activity, BN.com, was growing faster and was marketing its own e-reader, the NOOK.

Can dogs ever be revived? Rarely but not never and as the Rover/Jaguar examples shown above, they can at times not only be revived but can be re-established into a growing and successful businesses.

There are times when businesses are driven into this situation by bad management. Sometimes management simply loses sight of what's required. By looking at an existing business purely as a cash cow - once the cash flow starts to decline the view is that the business is about to die. This is often where private equity has a significant role and can acquire assets relatively cheaply and make a killing in the process. Odeon Cinemas was perceived as a dog. It was poorly managed, massively underinvested with a total loss of sight of what the consumer wanted. Under PE's ownership Odeon cinemas have been revitalised and re-invested in, with careful focus on what cinema-goers want.

Is the retail banking sector about to go through a period of structural change?

Revival usually is undertaken by a new leader and often by new owners. Revival within the same portfolio of businesses, within the same ownership by the same executive team is virtually unknown. It is a classic situation into which management consultants are called. What to do with underperforming assets? The recommendations have a large degree of similarity around the concepts of cutting out the dead wood and injecting a high dosage of change, subject to clarification and substantiation of market, demand and competitive potential.

Receivers are the professionals that deal with many dogs. In that respect they are the business world's equivalent of the undertakers. It's a tough job that requires no sentimentality at all, just total focus on ensuring all employees are managed with the utmost respect and professionalism, and that returns are maximised for creditors and shareholders - in that order.

From the website http://www.retailresearch.org/whosegone-bust.php a small selection of retailers that have died or been 'restructured' in the past couple of years include:

In 2012:

JJB Sports, the sportswear retailer with 180 stores, went into administration in September 2012. Sports Direct has bought its 20 best stores and other retailers have picked a few others up, but the rest have closed.

Peacocks, the fashion chain, posted a notice of intent to appoint an administrator covering the Peacocks chain and Bon-Marche. BonMarche was subsequently sold for £10m to Sun European Partners, although 160 stores closed.

La Senza, the lingerie retailer with 146 stores, announced at the end of December 2011 that it planned to enter administration in early Jan 2012 as part of a KPMG-planned company rescue.

Past Times, the modern antique-based business selling retro William Morris, Pre-Raphaelite etc merchandise, announced it planned to go into administration in Jan 2012. It previously went bust in 2005 and was acquired by Epic Private Equity. In 2010 it turned over £45m, but made losses of £1.5m.

Blacks Leisure, the outdoor sports, camping and recreational store, announced that after putting itself up for sale it had received no bids. The next stage is probably the sale of subsidi-aries, although a new bidder may still emerge. However, pre-pack administration is still likely to form part of the process.

The company has announced that its equity shares have little or no value at present.

In 2013:

Jessops, the only national UK camera retailer, was the first major retailer to go into administration in 2013. It had grown from around 50 stores in 1994, acquired Camera Crew and City Camera Exchange, and had more than 200 stores by 2002. It sold its central premises in 2008, avoided administration in 2009 by carrying out a debt for equity swap (involving HSBC taking 47% of its equity and a £34m debt write-off). The administrators closed down Jessops' 193 stores two days after taking control, partly at the instigation of Jessop's suppliers. Goods were returned to suppliers, who had become concerned that a 'fire sale' of under-priced merchandise by Jessops' would undermine everyone's businesses for the following few months.

Blockbuster, the national chain of video rental stores, went into administration in mid January. There are 528 stores with 4,190 employees. Like HMV, the chain was a former market leader, adversely affected by the importance of video downloads, online rentals and DVD sales.

HMV, the last UK chain of music and entertainment stores, went into administration after a weak Christmas and years of fighting a losing battle against downloads and online retailers. There are 238 stores. HMV is still trading though it is unlikely to attract a buyer for the whole business. The failure of HMV is likely to be a 'Woolworths moment' where shoppers (and no longer shoppers) realise that a changing world is exactly that.

Ethel Austin, the 32 remaining stores of the once-flourishing budget chain (which had 300 stores at one time), were closed immediately in January as the company went into administration for the fourth time. In July 2012, Liric bought 32 stores from the restructuring specialist GA Europe, but the company has been unable to continue.

Were all of the above dogs? Probably not, especially given that some elements of many have been saved. But all came to a stage when they simply could not continue to trade in their then state.

QUESTION MARK - by far the most complex situation to be in. These units exist because they were created for the massive potential that was assessed to be present in the market; the belief that overwhelming competitive advantages could be brought to bear, that stars were about to be born.

All new businesses are believed to be future stars. All new product launches and all new market entry strategies are believed to lead to stars. Whilst these investments are with the midwife they are question marks in that they are cash hungry, growing fast from small beginnings, but are within relatively small markets, or have only secured a small market share to-date.

As referred to in the earlier chapter, Tesco's Fresh & Easy investment in California, USA, was in this question mark category. The investment had consumed $1.4 billion of investment but was still generating a loss, and its future was far from certain. Tesco may have had a future star that could grow and mature into a cash cow, or they may have had something that developed into a dog for closure. We shall now never know as the decision was taken to dispose of it and write-off the investment and accumulated losses.

Tough nerves are required with such investments as well as thorough analysis of the realities of the situation. It may be appropriate to undertake a detailed SWOT analysis, to evaluate the likelihood of survival, but even with the most thorough analysis totally unpredictable events can create changes of such magnitude that the original plans and strategies have to be torn up, and the investment re-examined under a completely different set of assumptions.

In the *Financial Times*, 20th April 2011, (Lombard's column by Jonathan Guthrie), the following appeared:

"Fresh & Easy, Tesco's underperforming US groceries chain, bellies its name. There is nothing very fresh about a business that opened its first store in 2007. Nor has progress been easy: losses rose 13 per cent to £186m in the year to February 26. Break-even was originally pencilled in for 2010. That paradise has now been postponed until 2012-13."

It then goes on to state that Fresh & Easy pose's a real dilemma for Tesco's new CEO, Philip Clarke, who in his honeymoon period could make the decision, hard as it may be, to ditch the US operations. However, if he persisted with it for another year, the problems (or glories) would be associated with him and not his predecessor, Sir Terry Leahy - and frankly so it has been. Philip Clarke failed to call it on Fresh & Easy early in his tenure so its demise is now part of his legacy.

A couple of decades ago Marks & Spencer, the highly respected UK retailer, went on a large international growth surge. (Remember, the risks related to undertaking international expansion, even if you are a large and highly successful UK operator, are very significant. See chapter 4 on the Product/Market Evaluations Matrix). They expanded into France by opening their own stores. They expanded into the United States by acquiring the highly respected and successful American retailer Brooks Brothers. The board of Marks & Spencer authorised massive investments into these international growth projects. Both France and the United States remained as question marks within the company's portfolio of assets and over time continued to suck huge amounts of senior executives' time and cash. It was only after the departure of Sir Richard Greenbury, chairman and chief executive from 1988 to 1999, under whom Marks & Spencer undertook its greatest international expansion, that reality was faced and the question marks were faced up to as being unsupportable within the portfolio and divested of.

In 2007 I was chairman of a highly successful SME company called Coffee Point plc that was successfully sold to a UK FTSE 100 Company. Coffee Point grew into a leading vending company operating throughout the UK. It grew rapidly and profitably - predicated on one core principle, delivering quality in everything it did. The acquiring FTSE 100 company was a multi-billion pound corporation that had a miniscule vending operation (even though it was bigger than Coffee Point's) that it felt it could grow through acquisitions.

It became clear to me after a few years that the combined business wasn't working well - declining revenues and losses being incurred - so I approached the company and offered to buy it back. My offer was rejected out of hand, considered an insult and words to the effect: "we know what we're doing, we are big and successful and have the resources." In only another couple of years the company disposed of its entire vending operation registering a significant write down on the investment - the size of which could have been much smaller had they agreed to consider my proposal. The essence being that a star business, Coffee Point, was converted into a dog by incompetent management, lack of effective controls and investment and then was allowed to languish as a question mark as management simply were not prepared to face up to realities. Pride and ego have a lot to answer for.

As with dogs, a final decision on question marks usually requires new blood at board level to ensure that all sentimentality is removed and that the investments are given proper assessment for both what they are and what they are capable of becoming. If the analysis is that they are unlikely to be able to be turned into stars then stop the investment and divest. If on the other hand there is real potential for rapid growth and taking market share, then the investment should be continued and the asset retained.

The book retailer Waterstones was arguably in this situation. It was no longer a star, almost certainly not a cash cow, but not yet a dog. There was a potential acquirer. Waterstones' owner, HMV Group plc, had put out a number of 'profit warnings' indicating that the group was in difficulties. The acquirer came to the rescue and purchased Waterstones, giving it renewed life under new ownership. When EMI was acquired by Guy Hands' Terra Firma PE house it moved immediately into a question mark slot. The belief was that Guy Hands would be able to segment the assets and move some into star positions, some into cash cow positions and some into the dog sector to be disposed of, converting his investment into sizeable gains. Unfortunately it was not to be. It all went terribly wrong, incurring huge losses and write-offs and the clearing-up process of the complex set of EMI assets is still work-in-progress to some extent.

Sophisticated users of this matrix are able to overlay circles to indicate market size, arrows to indicate momentum/movement and generally increase the dynamic nature of the analysis and its representation.

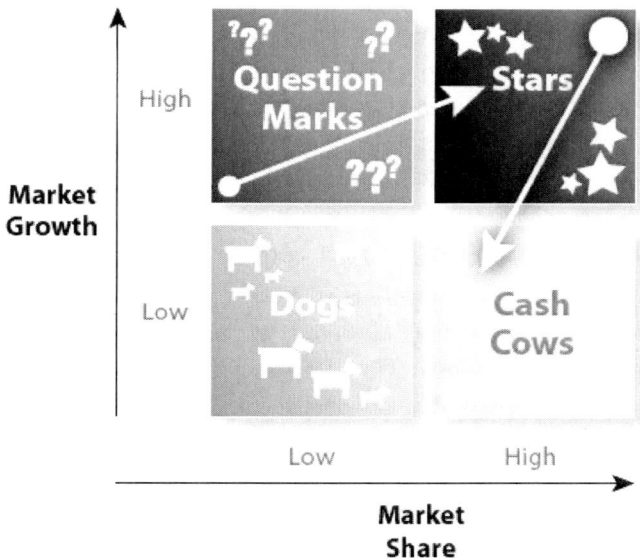

Market Growth

High

Low

Question Marks

Stars

Dogs

Cash Cows

Low   High

Market Share

For example, the above shows two products in movement, a star moving to cash cow, and a question mark moving towards a star positioning. If BlackBerry manages to regain consumer confidence and its new management team are able to bring a really competitive smartphone to market, it may well be able to move from question mark to star positioning yet again. If Apple's existing products range is successfully attacked by low-cost competitors, it is possible that it will move into a cash cow position, until it is able to regenerate - it already has a massive mountain of cash accumulated!

The matrix is commonly used in a number of diverse situations from corporate strategy to investment portfolio analysis.

But, a word of warning! As with all models, and especially as with all 2x2 matrices, they are aimed to present complex situations in a relatively simple, easily understandable format.

They are not either aimed to be all inclusive, nor all powerful. Their simplicity is their strength.

The Growth-Share model does not aim to suggest that market growth is the ONLY factor of an industry's attractiveness, or that relative market share is the ONLY factor to determine competitive advantage. It is using these two dimensions to illustrate the complex realities of the market place in a relatively simple 2x2 matrix. Its simplicity is its strength.

As I have mentioned a number of times, the absolute beauty of these matrices is exactly the fact that they are simple. As such they are able to break down complexity or help in the treatment of complex issues, and that is exactly what my final example aims to demonstrate. The famous 'Prisoner's Dilemma'.

Chapter 7
The Prisoner's Dilemma

Created in 1950 by Merrill Meeks Flood (1908 – 1991), with Melvin Dresher (1911–1992), while being at RAND, with Albert W. Tucker (1905 – 1995) giving the game its prison-sentence interpretation, and thus the name by which it is known today – the PRISONER'S DILEMMA. The matrix is based on fairly complex statistical analysis and aims to illustrate the likely outcomes from a number of different assumed scenarios. To do so the matrix is based on the assumption of two people being arrested for committing a defined crime, placed in individual cells and interrogated individually without being able to communicate with each other. The police are sure that the two arrested people have committed the alleged crime, but have no proof. They are therefore hoping to be able to obtain a confession from their interrogations.

The 'dilemma' for the prisoners is that neither knows what the other may or may not have said, and hence their thinking may be along the following lines:

- If Prisoner A confesses, he gets a reduced sentence and Prisoner B gets a full sentence (top right hand corner box).

- If Prisoner A trusts Prisoner B not to confess and keeps quiet, but Prisoner B does confesses, Prisoner A gets the full sentence, and Prisoner B gets a reduced sentence (bottom left hand corner box).

- If Prisoner A trusts Prisoner B not to confess and keeps quiet, and Prisoner B does exactly the same, they can both walk free (top left corner box).

- If both Prisoner A and Prisoner B confess, both get the full sentence (bottom right corner box)

In other words the outcomes are derived from classic game theory rules as win/win, win/lose and lose/lose.

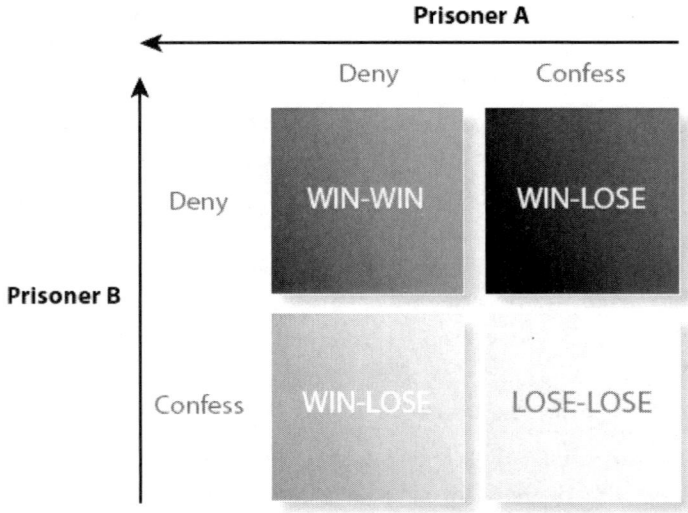

Or it can be shown in an even simpler, more visual format as below:

Prisoner's Dilemma (cc licensed (BY NC SA) flickr photo by Giulia Forsythe).

The complex statistical analysis that the above is based on is referred to as 'Decision Theory', which is defined by Wikipedia "as being concerned with identifying the values, uncertainties and other issues relevant in a given decision and the resulting optimal decision. It is very closely related to the field of game theory."

Prisoner's Dilemma has been depicted in many ways including the following cartoon:

All depictions show essentially the same set of potential outcomes.

Wikipedia goes on to show that there are "several statistical tools and methods... available to organize evidence, evaluate risks and aid in decision making."

"The risks of Type I and Type II errors can be quantified (estimated probability, cost, expected value, etc) and rational decision making is improved. One example shows a structure for deciding guilt in a criminal trial:"

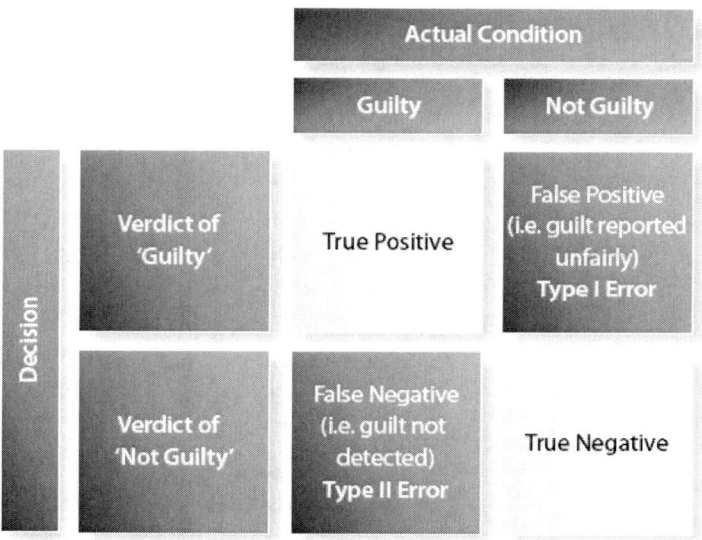

The above is identical to the Prisoner's Dilemma, but placed in a different setting. This simple variation demonstrates the power of this, and all of the 2x2 matrices included in this book.

The logic and simplicity, is applicable in an infinite number of ways to support thinking, analysis and decision-making.

Pricing acquisitions in complex competitive bidding situations is a classic example of where the above form of thinking can be applied.

At what price to pitch the offer? If too high, you may win but your shareholders may feel you overpaid to their disadvantage. If too low, you may lose to your competing bidders, and lose the assumed benefits of the acquisition.

In 1982 I was in exactly this type of situation when I was working as a senior executive with one of the UK's leading natural resource companies of the time, Consolidated Gold Fields plc. The company's main UK asset was a wholly owned subsidiary called Amey Roadstone Limited, the UK's second largest aggregate/construction material business. It became known that another company in the sector, a relatively large privately held aggregates business called Hoveringham Group, was up for sale. We undertook detailed analyses and our merchant bank advisers ran numerous models of what would be the right price to pitch our offer at. The Board of Gold Fields considered the advice they had received and made certain evaluations of their own. The key issue was exactly as above. We had determined that acquiring Hoveringham would be excellent for Amey Roadstone and would make the business the number one in its sector, but at what price? If we pitched the offer too high, how long before shareholders received a decent return? If too low, would we lose to other bidders? So what to do? We pitched it at what we assessed to be a generous price, but not too generous. We lost! The successful bidder, our principal competitor, Tarmac plc, paid significantly more than we had offered, and in retrospect they were right to do so. The acquisition turned out to be outstanding for the acquirer and generated significant shareholder value for them.

> "The acquisition of the Hoveringham Group in 1981 marked the company's entry into the brick, tile, building block and concrete markets. Hoveringham owned quarries in the United States and its takeover gave Tarmac a firm quarrying base in the United States."

> (http://www.fundinguniverse.com/company-histories/tarmac-plc-history/)

Of course, all such examples appear to be relatively easy decisions in retrospect, but at the time they consumed many hours of the Board's time and that of the professional advisers involved. Would the application of one of these matrices have been of value? Yes, without a doubt.

A much more recent example and one which has caused a lot of controversy is The Royal Mail's IPO in October 2013 at an initial price of 330p/share.

> "...Critics of Royal Mail's initial public offering (IPO) have attacked the government and its two 'global co-ordinators' Goldman Sachs and UBS, who advised the government on the privatisation, for undervaluing the communications firm. Its share price rocketed after the IPO and at the time of publishing sits at around 560p..."

> By Shane Croucher, November 28, 2013 10:59 AM GMT, International Business Times.

As the share price continued to perform well way past the period of initial offering, many seriously questioned the judgement of ministers who authorised the final strike price and that as a consequence all taxpayers have been short-changed! Easy in retrospect, but I guess the outrage would have been even greater had the IPO flopped!

Analysis can help, but in many situations you will be 'feeling' your way to what is the right position for your business. In many situations analysis helps provide the guidelines, but ultimately it comes down to the reality of 'willing buyer and willing seller'. In other words, undertaking detailed modelling and analyses will define the ball park you need to be in, but it usually comes down to what is the maximum you are prepared to pay, or the minimum you are prepared to accept, to close a deal. Exactly as per the example above with Amey Roadstone.

When one is bidding in an auction the same situation is taking place, albeit somewhat more transparent than sealed bidding. At an auction one is bidding against unknown others. The bidders have no sense of what limits others may have or how high they may be prepared to bid. The only thing each bidder knows in theory is their own limit. This is exactly the essence of an auction room. People get carried away by the desire of ownership, by the thrill of the chase, the overwhelming desire to win and not infrequently will bid way beyond their own 'set' limits just to obtain ownership of whatever they are bidding for.

Negotiations of all types lend themselves to the thinking provided by the conceptual framework of the Prisoner's Dilemma. When I worked in headhunting the negotiations around the securing of senior talent was very much in this space. The client defined the requirement in terms of expertise, experience, competencies, personality and the sort of compensation package that they were prepared to pay. As the headhunter, I then searched for candidates that best met the specification provided. Getting the client to agree to the terms asked for by the candidate and getting the candidate to agree to the terms offered by the client required a delicate process of negotiations. I heard clients say many times: "He's/She's bluffing... we don't need to enhance our offer... will not get a better deal anywhere else" etc. only to be confronted by an outright rejection. Of course it can happen the other way round too. The key is to have as good an understanding of the prevailing market, the candidate's perceived market worth and the extent to which the role impacts on business performance. Clearly the ideal scenario is one of win-win where one has an elated candidate believing that he/she has been highly professionally dealt with, with a package that has met or even exceeded expectations. For the company that's a candidate that exceeds their expectations in terms of gravitas, skills, expertise etc., a candidate that fits the senior team well, with good chemistry and a package that was within the remuneration committee's anticipated budget. It can happen.

Any situation involving negotiations between parties has numerous elements of the Prisoner's Dilemma. It's the unknown positions of negotiators that create the setting for the dilemma: push too hard and get into an intransigent position, accept too early and be damned by those being represented. Gaining agreement is to a large extent the win-win position that all negotiators ultimately want to get to.

BA's cabin staff dispute was a good example. It was an ongoing sore point both for the unions and for BA for a long time. It cost BA shareholders millions in lost profits and it cost BA cabin staff lost income and significantly lost goodwill amongst the fare-paying passengers. Yet the dispute took a very long time to resolve and how effectively it was resolved was highly questionable at the time.

It is in these types of situations that introducing Johari's Window just may help to overcome some of the more ingrained issues. The Prisoner's Dilemma may be helpful in setting out the prevailing set of circumstances and issues; Johari's Window may be introduced to gain some light on what both sides are trying to keep hidden, and by doing so may help to achieve real progress. In other words getting into a room and talking as openly as possible often times can unlock even the most intransigent situations.

After all, that is how peace was finally achieved in Northern Ireland and between Jordan, Egypt and Israel! If it can work in such complex and historically explosive situations, it can work anywhere. That is exactly how progress seems to have been achieved with Iran and its programme of nuclear capability development.

Chapter 8
Summary

This book has presented a small cross section of 2x2 matrices. These 2x2 matrices can have a potentially disproportionate impact on your businesses (and your own personal lives too).

I started with what, to me, is by far the most powerful of all 2x2 matrices, Johari's Window. This simple device:

- can so easily be applied in a vast number of varying situations;

- can be combined with a number of other matrices to facilitate analysis and resolution of complex issues;

- once understood, can help to overcome so many difficult instances of mis-understanding, mis-communication, or just plain lack of communication.

Engaging in dialogue, engaging in open one to one discussion, can be a lifesaver, and that's not an overstatement of the importance of the message within the matrix. Opening up the 'windows' into previously hidden/blind territories can help gain understanding.

In business the significance of better communication is well understood, especially as lack of communication is frequently highlighted as one of THE key issues within organisations. I cannot tell you the number of times both as a management consultant and as a non-executive chairman I have heard first hand that "management is simply not communicating enough/

effectively". This often may be true, but equally the problem is two sided in that neither management nor their employees were communicating enough. They simply failed to open their windows. I accept however, that it is up to management to initiate, to take the lead and encourage.

To communicate it is not enough just to talk. It is equally critical to listen. It is important that one listens actively - sending clear signals back to the speaker that one hears AND understands.

Many years ago I was asked to advise the senior executive team of a major Anglo-French corporation. There were real issues between two of the company's key divisions. Let's call them Division A (externally focused) and Division B (internally focused). Division A dealt with the businesses customers. Division B provided services that ensured that Division A had happy customers. So in reality Division A was Division B's customer - but no one saw it like that. To top it all, Division B's boss (a main board executive director) not only didn't see it like that either, but essentially locked himself away in his office issuing edicts, demanding people to come to him to report, but never ever went to 'his' customers to try to understand their actual needs/their expressed frustrations and problems.

When the analysis of the situation was presented I asked Division B's boss if he had any idea how he was perceived not only by his staff but also by others in the company? It was when I told him in private that he was called the 'Ice Man' that I got a real emotional response. He began to listen and take note. The windows began to open.

The net result was truly terrific. He:

- opened his door and left it open;

- started to walk to others and even walk around the plant to see and be seen, to engage in discussion, to ask 'how's it going?';

- implemented an 'internal customer' training programme for all his reports and the Division as a whole;

- implemented cross-divisional review meetings to ensure that 'his customers' were receiving the service level that they required.

This was fundamentally the result of having a consultant help to open his 'Johari's Windows'!

As I mentioned in the Johari's Window chapter, better and more open communication in one's personal life, aswell as business life, can overcome many frustrations, anxieties and just plain misunderstandings.

I then focused on the product/market matrix, again using the simplicity of the model to illustrate its effectiveness and value added in what are relatively complex situations. The reality is that they are real and everyday decisions that boards are required to make. Decisions to take a business into new markets, launch new products, or launch new products in new markets are decisions with huge implications. The related risks grow exponentially. The amount at stake financially can be equally massive. Gaining a better understanding of what's at stake aids the decision-making process and hopefully raises additional and possibly new questions along the way. Questions that aid making the right decision, although even the right decisions can be blown off course by subsequent unknowable events such as the virtual collapse of the world's financial markets in September/October 2008! Nevertheless the little product/market matrix helps to force your thinking, and that in itself is not a bad thing.

Companies often invest significant amounts of money on gaining as detailed an understanding of issues as possible before decisions need to be made. They employ the services of expensive investment bankers and management consultants. There is absolutely nothing wrong with this, but at times just a little internal questioning, just asking the 'whys', just a little self-testing of issues can be hugely beneficial. The 2x2 product/market matrix can be a powerful aid in this process.

Perhaps the best known and by far and the most widely used is the SWOT matrix, there are two key points I wanted to stress from the SWOT chapter:

1. That SWOT analysis can be used in a myriad of different ways and need not be considered exclusively for business units or companies. SWOT analysis can be applied to boards and management teams as well, with equal effectiveness.

2. The SWOT analysis can be combined with other 2x2 matrices to enhance the insights gained. For example, combining the information gained from SWOT with insights gained from Johari's Window. A powerful combination with significant potential benefits.

None of the above three matrices are either difficult to understand or difficult to apply. The next two were somewhat more complex both in terms of the concepts they are dealing with and their applications. They are still relatively simple 2x2 matrices, but the encompassing data and related models are more difficult to grasp.

The application of the imagery of Stars/Cash Cows/Question Marks/Dogs aims to simplify BCG's Growth-Share Matrix but the underlying analytical process is more complicated than that related to the previous matrices. The matrix also benefits greatly from the addition of other variables such as movement and relative size. By definition this third dimension adds to its perceived complexity and to its perceived value. Nevertheless, once grasped, this Growth-Share matrix, just like the preceding matrices, can become a relatively easy and hugely powerful tool for management. The Growth-Share matrix's key messages are clear: evaluate and understand your markets and your relative strengths within your markets. The basic take-away, as with all 2x2 matrices, is that complex issues can be broken down into relatively simple manageable compartments, evaluated and understood by the application of an appropriate 2x2 matrix or a combination of 2x2 matrices.

The same is true with the final matrix examined, The Prisoner's Dilemma. Essentially this is based on complex mathematical algorithms derived from decision theory. The presentation of the matrix in its simple win/win; win/lose; lose/lose format provides the simplification inherent in 2x2s.

Remember that the application of any of these and other matrices is an aid to decision-making, NOT the solution. They are dependent on the quality of the input as much as any analytical process. The old notion of 'garbage in, garbage out' is just as true here as anywhere! But, if used appropriately, they are powerful devices and powerful learning aids too.

I have deliberately not made this into a textbook and have kept each of the chapters relatively short. I have deliberately restricted the number of matrices introduced and outlined to just five in total. I have deliberately used contemporary examples to bring to life the relevance and value of each of the matrices outlined.

2x2 matrices are simple to construct, simple to use, simple to apply and have an amazing ability to simplify what otherwise may be considered complex and what otherwise can be complex. How you use either the matrices contained in this book or the myriad of others that already exist is clearly up to you. Or indeed you may wish to apply the 2x2 thinking and create your own models. (It is fair to say that there are a vast number of other matrices, 3x3, 4x4... etc, however in this book I have focused on the most popular and for me the most useful in the form of 2x2 matrices.)

That is by far the most important result I hope this book may have achieved. For you to have gained enough confidence and understanding to be able to apply 2x2 matrices to your own situation.

As I stated right at the beginning of this book, only the limits of your own imagination constrain the application or development of 2x2 matrices. Only the limits of your will to engage constrain the use of these simple tools for the benefit of your business.

Again, as already referenced, if you Google '2x2 matrix' a world of imagination and opportunity opens up, demonstrating the unlimited potential available!

The fact is, they are simple, they are easy to use and they are of great help in an immense number of diverse situations.

Do it, do it now!